# BEYOND THE SEA

## ODYSSEY

John T. Eber Sr.

MANAGING EDITOR

A publication of

Eber & Wein Publishing

Pennsylvania

Beyond the Sea: Odyssey
Copyright © 2015 by Eber & Wein Publishing as a compilation.

Library of Congress
Cataloging in Publication Data

ISBN 978-1-60880-409-2

Proudly manufactured in the United States of America by

Eber & Wein Publishing
Pennsylvania

# A Note from the Editor . . .

But we'll never do aught, I know, unless
We are brave as our sires of old,
And face like them the bitterness
Of the battle and storm and cold;
Unless we boldly stand,
When men would hold us back,
With the helm-board in our hand,
And our eyes to the shining track
Of what may be
Beyond the sea.

—Frederick George Scott
*from* "Knowledge" (1887)

Welcome, poets and readers. Over the past year I have diligently read your work, seen your joy, and felt your pain. I'm not alone in that experience for here we meet together again, between these covers, where we may run free and speak words dearest to us. Some of us obscure our identities, but we all bare our souls in these humble pages.

We are from all walks of life and we come together here to share with mutual respect our creations from beginners to seasoned veterans. Poets write about life gained and life lost, tragedies, outrage, transitions recognized, seasons celebrated, a year's worth of holidays, prescriptions for change, advice for the future, dreams, wonderlands, landscapes of melancholy, new love, old love, crushing heartbreak, creatures fair and ferocious, childhood memories, lifelong pursuits, and passionate spirituality. No topic is off-limits or ignored.

Life is sometimes cold, mechanical, and unforgiving, but we have love, art, and poetry to emancipate our spirits. Beauty woven with language can reconnect us with those we've lost. Verse can ring out the adoration we feel deep inside. Poetry can be a manifestation of playful, carefree whimsy. This beauty hides in all of us and takes a multitude of forms. Some poets exercise careful structure in their work while others employ a more organic composition. Rhyming or not, poems capture language as a living entity and give simple printed words vivacious energy.

Above all, this book is a record, a time capsule even, in which we can revisit the past, dream about the future, and reach our children's children. Verse has waned in public opinion, perhaps with the elevated pace of modern life, but its importance is still as vital, and it is here we take up that meaningful work.

Poetry permits us to tell our stories, heal from our pain, and celebrate our successes; it is a vital form of communication, a necessity of the human condition. The task does not always come easy, and may require the bravery Frederick George Scott describes above, but the reward is release, relief, and accomplishment. The same can be said for reading, too; can a story be told if no one hears it? Poetry is a hallowed covenant between writer and reader—one cannot exist without the other. Writers must read as much as readers need to venture out with their own voice.

Thank you, steadfast readers, and thank you, poets—I extend my deepest appreciation to all for keeping poetry alive and opening your hearts and confiding your experiences from which we may all learn and grow. Look with me now, beyond the sea, to what new adventures we will brave! May your pen always flow swiftly across the page. You have made history.

Desiree Halkyer
Editor

# I Choose Not to Hold Pain

Did you mean to send that arrow with the words you said?
My hand couldn't help to cover the hole but the red still showed,
if so I will feel sorry for where you're at in life today,
but in time I will forgive and let go of the words you said,
because in my heart I don't want to hold this pain.

Or did you second guess what you said but said it anyway?
That at least slows the pain down on my part to catch my breath,
this I can understand for haven't I been there a time or two,
but in time I will forgive and let go of the words you said,
because in my heart I don't want to hold this pain.

Maybe it was not intentional on your part the words you said,
maybe you didn't know with your words an arrow landed in
    my heart,
this I can understand aren't I guilty of saying things in ignorance,
but in time I will forgive and let go of the words you said,
because in my heart I don't want to hold this pain.

Though I feel it was intentional on your part those words you said,
and relying on my intuition the odds are I'm right to feel this way,
this I will struggle and wrestle with in order to forgive,
but in time I will forgive and let go of the words you said,
because in my heart I choose not to hold this pain.

Cynthia June Pinto
*Whiting, NJ*

## Sweetheart

I like the way you stand and walk
I like the way you softly talk
Oh, to see that twinkle in your eyes
It moves me just to see you smile

As the trees sway in the morning breeze
Where you are, I want to be
As the ocean swells with the tide
I want you sweetheart by my side

I have never felt this way before
I love you and, I want you to know
I dream of you, most every night
I want you to kiss me and hold me tight

May the stars shine with all their charm
Enough to keep you in my empty arms
May the moon light in the sky: whisper too
I can't be happy until I be with you

Johnnie Chaney
*Macon, GA*

## Stain

my reflection blurs as I pass the mirrored wall
the stain of my presence lingers on the glass
for all
for no one

my identity unique like the print on my fingers
naked and vulnerable to all that know me
no one knows me
I don't know me

my boundaries choking the life from my visions
absent of breath the light fades to black
no one sees me
I am transparent

my mortality questioned as I ponder this state of mind
this rush that enables my existence
no one is waiting
I am alone

my heart broken and its pieces pierce my flesh
the pain lost in translation
no one notices
I am silent

Karen Sandberg
*River Falls, WI*

## My Family

My family means so very much,
We often try to keep in touch;
Some in one place, some another,
But we remain as sisters and brothers.

We communicate often by telephone,
Especially when I feel alone.
To hear a voice so soothing and kind.
Don't disconnect, stay on the line.

My family is my hope for tomorrow
We can share each other's sorrow;
Take the time and come together,
Whether fair or stormy weather.

What does your family mean to you?
I hope and pray you can say too;
We've grown more close year by year,
For this I need not shed a tear.

Laughing, loving and praising God too,
He is willing to see us through;
So don't forget the family altar,
It will help to calm rough waters.

Cherish the moments you have left,
Taking advantage while you have breath,
To embrace each other with love and affection.
Thank God my family has true connections.

Dorris Nesbitt
*Brooklyn, NY*

*This is one of the poems I was inspired to write during a one-month period. During this period I penned eighty-six poems. The words were coming so fast, my hand could hardly keep the pace. God is my inspiration. At the age of eighty-three, God is still adding to my numerous talents. I am hoping that this poem in some way will help to uplift someone's spirit.*

## Aeronautics

The sky, a sea.
A flotation's floor of cumulous
crystals vapors pour.
Airlifts of jet streams,
updrafts flow.
Blues awash in ocean's indigo.
Our stratosphere of frosted froth.
Here a speck slithers slowly,
silently aloft.
A speck, a slender thread with trails
so drawn. Its needling's luster of silver
tailings prong.
Four thousand maiden voyages,
these flights, with wings,
with wishes quest, ascend
to heights.
These corners of our compass round.
For to, for fro, lo heavens bound.
Bliss of solitude, supreme domain.
Toast princely Pegasus, of laurels,
and legends, where lofty pilots reign.

Edward Schoeffler
*Chicago, IL*

*In March of 2008, I received the International Library of Poetry Editor's Choice Award for "A Cradle of Care"—dedicated to mothers, "Playlot"—delirium style, "Fears, Phantoms and Frailty." "Calendar" required two years to complete and 246 revisions. Unpublished "Aeronautics" is about majestic high altitude flight, dedicated to the United States Air Force Academy. I am seventy-four years of age.*

# Sometimes

Sometimes things can happen in your life,
Things that make you *stop!* and wonder why,
Things that make you feel so lonely,
Things that make you want to cry;
But always know that there's someone who needs you,
Always know that there's someone who cares,
Always know that there's someone who loves you,
Lonely, but never alone.
A loss, a debt, a tragedy,
A happening that shouldn't be,
Can leave you feeling so alone,
Not knowing where to turn.
But always know that there's someone who needs you,
Always know that there's someone who cares,
Always know that there's someone who loves you,
Lonely, but never alone.
So when those sometimes come your way,
As we all know they will,
Just open up your heart.
And you will find that someone
Whose always been there.
So always know that there's someone who needs you,
Always know that there's someone who cares,
Always know that there's someone who loves you,
Lonely, lonely, but never alone.

Gregory Magyar
*Cox's Creek, KY*

*Several years ago, I lost my wife of twenty-four years very suddenly and the loss left a big hole in my life and I felt very alone. Although we were not blessed with children of our own we both loved being around them and this made our love for each other even stronger. I have since remarried and became part of a "blended family" as my new wife had three teenage children. On the birthday of my first grandchild twelve years ago, I wrote this poem to share the joy of knowing that no matter what the happenings in one's life, there is always someone who needs you, someone who cares, someone who loves you and if you believe, you may feel lonely but you will never truly be alone.*

# The Davenport

She would kneel on the davenport, my grandmother,
   her elbows propped on its back, her head resting on prayer-
   folded hands,
   and watch, watch out the window.
Always, it was when the sun brush-stroked the sky
   at the seam between day and night.

She said she hated sunsets.
   The one man she loved with her soul
   walked out on her at sunset.
And so she watched through golds and reds,
   not for his return, but for his memory.

Years later, my mother too would kneel on the davenport
   in the same manner and at the same time of day,
   and wait, wait.
At the faintest sound of a motor, her watching would swing to
   the distant auto
   as if she could pull it closer with her eyes.

Each time, as the sound crescendoed, then faded into long
   shadows,
   she'd twist the ring on her left hand.
   Sometimes she got her wish.
Sometimes my father came home on time.

Now I kneel on the davenport
   just when the sky, like a great, cosmic mating bird,
   displays with swirls of lilac and rose and emerald.

For that one moment, the pain of my mothers subsides for me,
   and something in me yearns, yearns.
I rest my head on a ringless hand
   and wonder what I have missed.

Holly Lee Vecchio
*Alhambra, CA*

## Is Hard Work the Way of Life?

When the case in point
To work your bones to the joint
And be all stressed out
Of all the traffic on the route.

Then take a deep breath
And seek life not death
Learn the *way* from Jesus
And with what He feeds us.

For His relationship is easy and
Peaceful work
Omitting melon collie and torque
Not asking too much
And the such.

Sims G. Dildy Jr.
*Texarkana, AR*

*I live according to "the sermon of the mount." Life will get to be too much to handle, so Jesus tells us to come to Him at that point. When I step out to join Him, the world does not understand and dopes you up in a mental hospital. It seems the world wants to know what you learned from the "boss."*

# Let's Go Home

March 7, 2013
A plain old day you'd say
And so it seemed to us
As we went along our way

Well it really was a special day
But was it good or bad
It really hinged upon a test
That our loved one had

Today I realized
That money's not the thing
For I felt real happiness
By what a smile can bring

We waited in the doctor's room
What would the answer be
He came in and smiled and said
Good news you're cancer free

Leonard Borello
*Saratoga, CA*

## HH-60 Jayhawk

Did you hear the helicopter—
I wrote the message on birch bark—
it sounded like the cry of a long-tailed
tyrant limping along like the
main rotor blade was too short,
spinning its ellipsis.
Did you pray?
The voice on the other line
spoke Novocaine—
and I could see through
skin tight starlight
a fossil-engine animal
above a tree line. The voice said
it is not for you to know when
watermelon will bleed the darkest.
I had been standing in the stench
of the faltering sun when I heard it.
I went inside, shut the drapes,
and took off my watch.

Jacob Miller
*Upper Saddle River, NJ*

*Human thought—how bold, how brazen. This is a much longer answer than you were bargaining for but it will be quite natural when there is only silence and desperation walks in the springtime. It will finish in the summer but for now it seems too dangerous, a shell to the ear, because I have been haunted by something not just a lonely little anomaly. I do not need to be protected. I am not porous. I have come from nothing, a quivering expectancy that I could read bodies and hear the trumpets of the world around me, made radiant from far, far away.*

# Fear

Fear is false evidence against the righteous
It renders a verdict that unto you there is no justice!
Fear hath torment… it is hell-sent
Demons can't attack God, so they use the human to vent
Fear is Hell's adhesive… stay there and you won't live!
Fear stops you from going forward, you remain stagnant
Your new BFF (best friend forever) is now a magnet!
Instead of saying "Hi!" you greet with a Hell-O (Hell low)
Fear's seeds are planted on Lodibar's soil, so you can't even grow!

One of life's challenges is fear
Undaunted with its nose in the air
It travels anywhere
Without prejudice or racism, without care!

So much has been said about the bloodsucking bed bug
But did you hear about the bugbear?
For real!
It's the life sucking fear
So stand clear
The extermination is free and near

Dial 1-800-GOD-FEAR!
That's the fear of the Lord
No more bugbears—you and peace are now on once accord
Fear is cast out by perfect love…
This is a decree sealed by the holy trio from above!
Fear exterminators—Yahweh, Jesus, the Holy Ghost

Deidrea Woods
*Brooklyn, NY*

*I am the youngest of four girls. I graduated with a MS in elementary education from the City College of NY. About five years ago, I heard the Lord tell me, "Fear not," and the Spirit led me to read, meditate and pray on Isaiah 43: 1–21. I read it, but did not meditate or pray on it! I lived in fear and dread almost every day. After failed suicide attempts, God took me right back to what he said, in the beginning: Isaiah 43: 1–21 and he added a bonus, Isaiah 54: 1–17. Read it, meditate on it, and pray without ceasing.*

## Smiles

Put a smile upon your face.
　　Make where you are a happy place.
It's good for others, and for you.
　　It's such a pleasant thing to do.

It doesn't cost a dime to smile,
　　And it's very worth your while.
You'll find your day will go much better.
　　A smile is such a good pace setter.

A smile can make a heart feel glad,
　　And cheer you up when you are sad.
It can brighten up a rainy day,
　　And make December feel like May.

A friendly smile reflects God's love.
　　It's like a blessing from above —
Just like a ray of warm sunshine,
　　And always welcome any time.

So smile at someone on your way,
　　And say you wish them a happy day.
You just may find a brand new friend,
　　Or help a lonely heart to mend.

Christine O'Rear
*Rossville, GA*

*I am an eighty-one-year-old great-grandmother. I started writing poetry sixteen years ago. It seemed to help me with grief, loneliness and all those problems that crop up after the death of a spouse. Then I started writing just for the enjoyment of it. I write about everyday thoughts and events and about special occasions and family—some serious, some fun. My present husband and I are enjoying our "golden" years together with family, church and friends. We like to garden, feed the birds and travel a little.*

# The Wilderness

I am in this wilderness with not a soul around
I keep walking and searching for a way out, but there isn't one to be found
Is there an end to this journey you planned for me all along?
I keep hearing "soon" but I am afraid that "soon" is even too long
I feel the weight of this and I have been fighting so hard all this time
Keeping my faith and my courage throughout all this struggle of mine
But I am really feeling the weight of this very strong now
I don't know if I can muster my foot off the ground
To take another step without some peace
I cannot rest when I cannot see
Help me to understand that I am fighting for something better than this
That there will be an end to all of this
I will walk with you through anything as I know you are always there
I just need some encouragement to keep going; I need you to show me that I am almost there
To what you have planned for me
For what you are crafting me to be
I know you are always listening and I know that you care
I know I'll look back and then understand the whole plan
I will continue to have faith throughout it all
I will keep my eye on you and know that you will be there even when I fall

Angela Cullen
*Sherwood, AR*

# Please Remember

The time last summer, can you forget?
The nights, the moonlight — I remember yet.
Your eyes, your lips, the touch of your hand
Now those nights are gone — but they were grand
The fields, the lanes, the places we'd go
All are gone now buried under the snow.

I sit and sigh, the teardrops fall.
Please, please don't say you don't recall
Or say that you can care no more
You couldn't forget when you cared before
Your tender kisses, your warm embrace.

Soon the fields will be green again — spring will return
And deep within my heart will burn
The want for you, the need for you
Can you really say that you don't want me too?
Your kisses sweet, your arms so strong
I ask that you remember — was it really all so wrong?

Mary Jane MacLaughlin
*Schuylkill Haven, PA*

*I am a rural Pennsylvanian recently retired after a long career in an educational setting. I've been married for thirty-six years and while we live in the country, our daughter, son-in-law and new granddaughter live in another country, Italy, a different and exciting place. Spending time with our Italian family is something I truly enjoy, as are dancing, Zumba, traveling and writing poetry. I've loved to compose poems since I was a teenager, and hope to write more in retirement. Poetry requires use of creativity and imagination, and encourages dreaming freely, to express, seemingly magically, the innermost feelings of the soul.*

## Growing Old

His eyes were dim,
  He could hardly see
I'm old he said softly,
  But the Lord blesses me.

His back is bent over,
  He drags his feet,
His hands shake too,
  But his manner is sweet.

How old is he? Someone asked.
  One hundred and two was the reply.
But one day soon I'll be at
  My home in the sky.

There will be mansions of
  Gold and gates of pearl.
The Lord himself I'll see,
  And this wretched body will be made new.

Bless the Lord, He has redeemed me!

Marjorie Creel
*Raleigh, NC*

## The African Ebola

Oh mother Africa, here you come again with Ebola
You generated AIDS from the Ugandan monkeys
Whose pains and pangs we still live with
Now you've played around with Liberian monkeys
And hatched this terrible Ebola

Fool me once, shame on you
Fool me twice, shame on me
AIDS travelled so fast globally
Ebola what is your pathway?
You've refused to stay in your jungle Africa

Stay away from international airplanes
What are you doing in Dallas?
Watch your steps in Atlanta
Get off the corridors and gates of "the Big Apple"
Atlanta, Chicago, Los Angeles, New York and Washington:
   when in doubt, quarantine

Oh Humane Society, evangelist, and preachers
Which one takes precedence, monkeys or humans?
Ebola, you've downed 5,000 lives and counting
The monkeys are still alive and thriving
You rebuff court orders, intimidate Red Cross and health
   personnel alike

Oh God of all creations
Monkeys are making a mockery of your creation
Hurry to our rescue and remedy us humans
Let not monkeys inherit this your earth alone
Please, please solve this puzzle once and for all

Chima Agueze
*Round Rock, TX*

## Spellbound

When shadows fall on starry nights,
Soft moonlight casts a spell.
The world is filled with wondrous sights,
When shadows fall on starry nights.
The evening promises delights,
As all lovers can tell.
When shadows fall on starry nights,
Soft moonlight casts a spell.

Joan Patterson Yeck
*Moosic, PA*

*I live in Moosic, PA—Northeastern PA—with my husband, Bob. We have four children, Michelle, Nicole, Rob and Mike, and a grandson, Matthew. I have been writing poetry since I was twelve years old. Since we had our children, I have also written lullabies and children's stories and songs for them and our grandson. They and my husband all share my love for writing. I especially love to write in the triolet and haiku forms and find inspiration from my family and friends, nature, songs, lyrics and even hymns. Reading and writing poetry are my favorite forms of relaxation.*

## Autumn

I've longed for the return of the cool nights,
And dreamed during the sunny, warm school days,
Of the shiny, bright, humming football lights,
And the frightful fall nights full of dusty haze.

Flaming bonfires and toasting marshmallows,
Make for a night filled with friends and much fun.
Frightening ghost stories, and all hallows,
Are told during nights, darkened with no sun.

Leaves with colors of orange, yellow, and red,
Create a colorful canvas of art.
The beautiful autumn hues are all toasted,
For all artists' masterpieces to start.

Autumn colors, tried and true, fun and friends,
Create this time of year, which will soon end.

Paige Farris
*Kinston, AL*

*Paige Farris is a senior at Geneva High School and she is seventeen. Her parents are Brad and LyDonna Farris and her sister is Haley Farris who is fourteen.*

## Sally Tonight

Sally tonight by candlelight
To ocean gleam and glimmer.
To mournful cries of ocean sighs.
Where city lights grow dimmer.

Roses cling to craggy rocks
Inky black tamaracks
Seaweed hissing on the shore
Follow old and faded tracks

Now I see the shimmering waves
Playful foam like little cats
Snatch the sand upon the shore
Then bits of driftwood follow that.

Only gentle breezes stay
Comes in fog thick and white
Telescoping all my dreams
And closing in the night.

Joyce Tartamella
*Jensen Beach, FL*

## Sorry

Please don't say sorry — I don't like that word —
I hear it so often, it sounds quite absurd.

You think that a sorry absolves and can heal?
It's your verbal eraser… it's nothing you feel.

Just an abracadabra you practice in vain —
That same hollow sorry — again and again.

An emotional blindfold when spoken by you —
A flimsy failed fabric that I can see through.

Well, I am now sorry: and sorry to say —
I am sorry — most sorry: I am going away.

Lorna Moir
*Maitland, FL*

*I was born in Johannesburg, South Africa (nee du Preez). I came to Florida,
USA, in 1992 and am a happy, naturalized American. I think I have the secret to
good emotional and physical health: express it in verse and dance around the house.*

# Tired Old Man

Grandpa works all day long. Old but strong and
gray-headed.
Stronger than an ox.

69 years old building a house. Gets tired but doesn't stop.

He could break his back like he has done before, but he doesn't stop.
Grandma tries to help but she is old and works all day long.
But I try to help but I can't, because gigantic cherry beams
that look like long rugged logs that I can't lift.

He doesn't pay or hire nobody to help. He says he can
do it all by himself.

I don't know how he does it, but he sure doesn't stop. Tired
old man he is.

Brandon Devault
*Gordonsville, VA*

*I, Brandon Devault, spent fifteen years of my childhood, on weekends, with Arnold
Mundy — my grandpa. He was the greatest inspiration in my life. He taught me
to save, to use "hands-on experience," education, to be honest, respectful, and help
those in need, and he took me to church. We went camping and fishing, and he
built me a play house, along with my help. We planted trees and had a garden.
We did all of the above along with "Grandma," Mary Mundy. He built the house
I wrote the poem about. He built me a room, it is a huge A-frame house, the entire
loft was mine. It remains with my "things." I am now twenty-four years old — I
live in Orlando, FL. Grandpa is buried in Culpeper, VA, military cemetery. He
passed on May thirteenth, 2011.*

## Friends

The little white kitten and the little black dog
  Went to play with the little green frog.
They played and they played till the sun went down,
  That's when the kitten nearly drowned.

She spit and she sputtered 'cause she couldn't swim,
  But she followed the frog when he jumped in.
She called to the dog who wouldn't believe her,
  He could swim, he was a lab retriever.

Now the moral of the story is, you better skedaddle
  If you don't know how to do the doggy paddle!

Irene M. Morgan
*Ashland, PA*

# From My Eyes

From my eyes
All I saw was a hand waving.

I don't understand why you left.
This is the hardest time in my life.

I need you now because without you I am lost.
Only teardrops burn in my eyes.

I heard that you are going to India.

Tell me why?

I forgot.
It is not your choice or mine.

Time and time again you just walk out of my life.
Why don't you ever stay?
Is this really forever?

Forever leaves no room for hope.
You have been a part of my life — since the very beginning.

Before you go I wanted to tell you how much I love you.
Only now, the words are imprisoned in my soul.

I learned so many things from you:
To be warm-hearted, to be loving, kind and caring.
This is your special gift to me.

I wish I could go to India with you.
But, I can't.
My life is here in America.

As I saw the clothes being packed... my heart shrivelled and
Filled with sadness.
My eyes were swollen with so many tears.

Varsha Saxena
*Palo Alto, CA*

## A Sonnet to Jim

Now that you are gone and we must say a forever farewell,
Life will never be the same as I miss you and bewail.

For without you my heart cries tears of sorrow, and
For that I hold no shame today and for all tomorrows.

Because our love was so special and deep,
There will be enduring memories to keep.

Finding you enriched my life,
It was an honor to be your wife.

Through the years we were also best friends,
And I will love you until my own life ends.

You will always live on in my heart, and
It gives me comfort to hold you close as I make a new start.

No one could ever take your place,
Because our love transcends both time and space.

Poet H. Hartmann-Phipps
*Reeds Spring, MO*

*I attended the Chicago Art Institute on scholarships. I've received awards by local art councils, a second prize for a Chicago city-wide essay contest, and I have been an environmental advocate since my late teens. I promote protection of our natural resources, and one of my environmental articles was read on the floor of the Missouri State Senate. I also promote women's rights, animal rights, and natural health. Though the focus has always been editorial comments covering various issues, Jim was the one who inspired me to also write poetry. His daughters and I celebrate this amazing man!*

## Who's Old?

I was told that I look old
I am only 21 as you can see
If you see someone that's old
It isn't me
On my head
I don't have one grey hair
And I don't have a wrinkle anywhere
Why must someone be so bold to
Tell me that I am old?

Marvin Goldfarb
*Sunnyside, NY*

## Not Too Perfect Anymore

The filth of gray has touched her head,
Skin, riven with light lines;
Once lithe, her figure lags behind where it was pert.
But, oh! She is sought after in the boardroom after bright repartee…
At night no one reaches past the less than perfect body in bed.
Cracks form on both sides of a mouth no ones kisses
As she remembers what it was like to be embraced in sleep, in
    dreams, in love…
A single tear stains her perfect pillow,
Again.

Meryl Taylor
*Connecticut, OH*

# Live

Walking a lonely road
No destination in mind
Going where the wind takes me
Trying, just trying, to get through
Make it through life in one piece
Not broken, not torn, not cracked
I want to live my life
I don't want to just survive
I want to love
I want to care
Want to know
Want to share
To understand
To give
Learn
Laugh
But most of all, just to live
Live my life to the fullest
The fullest it can be
Nothing to regret
Nothing to lose
Everything to love
Everything to gain

Alexandria VanOrd
*Warren, PA*

# I Wish You Could See What I See

I wish you could see what I see
The beautiful sunrises illuminating
The morning sky
Subtle hues of yellow, pale blue
Bright pink and orange

I wish you could see what I see
Mist rising off the ponds
Clouds reflected on the mirrored surface
Of the lake
Gorgeous mountains, waterfalls, wildlife

I wish you could see what I see
Wherever I have journeyed you have been with me
I have shared with you through my writings,
My pictures and my words
You listened intently and gave me a smile
I have taken you along in my dreams
Hand in hand

You have always been with me
In my heart and in my thoughts

I wish you could see what I see
How special you are to me

Patrick Mahon
*Newton, NJ*

## Lover

I could watch
a thousand suns
rise over as
many seas,
if I could
look at you
each time
and know that
you still cared
for me
But if I found
that your feelings
had changed
I'd turn my back
to the sun
seeing only
sunless forest
and noiseless
shadows…

Susan Mellberg
*Byrnes Mill, MO*

*My name is Susan Mellberg. I was born in Springfield, MA. Later, I moved to St. Louis, MO. I started writing poetry as a child. I have many other poems. This poem I wrote in the midst of my divorce. He was the love of my life and became ill and has now recovered. I believe poetry, for me, is an extension of myself. It includes all things around you and a true love for life. I'm so honored to be in this book.*

# Story of the Broken Heart

There was a man, lost without love, bounded by sorrow.
He wished for love, hoping for tomorrow.
A lonely man distressed by his emotions,
living day to day with his mental commotions.
A tender heart hurt many a time.
Wanting to love, was it a crime?
"When will love come?"
"Soon?"
"Is it near?" cried this lonely young man
of his sorrowful cheer.
After years of rejection, bitterness, and pain,
he fell asleep one day to the sound of the rain.
He did this at times to dream and escape
From his emotional scars and emotional rape.
Little did he know that this sleep was forever,
and that this was the end of his personal endeavor.
An autopsy was performed to find his heart split in two.
The doctors and nurses thought, "Could this be true?"
For the records they didn't know where to start.
So the final record read:
"Died of a broken heart."

Dino Dickson
*Beaver Falls, PA*

## S. O. S.

We all need help at times
But we don't like to admit it
The guilt of it feels likes chimes
We all know we sin
And we are all basically kin
So let's save our souls together
Let's save our souls together

Amber Seward
*Wichita Falls, TX*

## A Writer's Madness

You have to be arrested for writing this arresting piece of work.
Whether or not your amazing body of work that you put down on
   canvas is pure brilliance or insanity,
Is up to the interpretation of the reader.
A person should put a "Don't Disturb" sign on the writer's door.
Please, don't disturb genius at work.
Now, how's that for poetic food for thought?
The poet Dante was banished when he wrote *The Divine Comedy*.
Was he banished for his poetic creativity
Or his imaginary insanity of what he thought that hell was like in
   his divine classic?
Oh, what hells we go through as a writer?

Christopher Taylor
*Montclair, CA*

# Love a Daddy

My thoughts drift back to years ago—streetcars, Broadway, twins
in tow.
The Tomboy store, our home above—laughter always filled with love.
I still can hear the cheerful sound—accordion music all around.
The "fresh eggs" store amazed me so—chickens running to and fro.
I loved "Ted Drewes"—a special treat, on Friday night to beat
the heat.
Cape Cod was heaven in my mind; by train or car, rock walls to find.
Our Nobska Beach, the shells, the sand—an inner tube, my
daddy's hand.
I felt so safe with Daddy close. Besides my twin, I loved him most.
Blond hair, blue eyes, with ruddy skin—my dad, my hero, best of kin.
Musician, officer, and "Doc"—his energy was hard to mock.
He built a swing set in our yard; with work and study, it was hard.
Determination got him through a life of troubles—not a few.
Soft-spoken, gentle—that's my dad, and yet I fear to make him mad.
He's kind and giving, lends an ear. His life experience makes
him dear.
I could go on forevermore about my dad, my friend.
He's in my heart, an endless love, not even death can end.
The memories too numerous can be summed up this way—
Your daughter loves you and proclaims this "Love a Daddy" day!

Carol Krigbaum
*Warrenton, MO*

*Carol Krigbaum, a graduate of Hannibal-LaGrange University, is a retired surgical coordinator with three children, three grandchildren and one great-grandchild. Each of her poems was inspired by different family members, including pets. Thirty-two poems have resulted. Carol and Ron, her husband of fifty years, live in a retirement community on a lake. They love their home on the water and feel as if they are "on vacation" all year long.*

## Witch's Teeth

Halloween time is here
Scary ghosts, witches and pirates
Happy and having fun
Going from house to house
Oh no it's Frankenstein and werewolf
A mummy just ran by
Oh please let me stop and rest
I am scared to death
Daddy I'm glad you're here
See the witch that just flew by
The witch went to the harvest moon
I thought she was coming for me
She wants my candy
She wants me to share
The witch's teeth are falling out
She needs no candy at all
Shall I tell her to brush her teeth
Maybe we should pull them out
If we pull them out she might give a loud shout
She might stay on the moon
She might fly away on her broom
But no she won't fly away
She won't stay on the moon
She won't give a loud shout
She'll just eat and eat until the rest fall out

Peggy Alden
*Springfield, OH*

## Tummy Rub

Licking her paws, basking in the sun filtering through the window,
Patti melted into her relaxation.
Occasionally she'd chase a sun beam, and then melt back into
  her compensation.

Her green, emerald eyes would glance around for a human post to
  purr against.
Spotting her target, she meandered to her master, rolled over,
  presenting her tummy for a rub.

A gleeful smile took over her face when massaged. She was
  no dummy.
White cat whiskers quivered in ecstasy.
Catnip was no match for the rub of her tummy.

Pauline Greene Bulko
*Greenfield, MA*

## That Summer Day

A summer day in mid-July, a ringing telephone,
A time arranged, a step into a venture yet unknown.

The radiance of the July sun, a noonday rendezvous,
The locusts hummed in vibrant tones in trees of emerald hue.

So it began…

A trek of dual desire to wander from the path of solo flight
And fill a void with warmth, and touch, and smell and closeness in
    the night.

The nights… quiet sometimes, and sometimes filled with wild and
    crazy fun!
And passion sometimes much akin to the heat of the summer sun.

And tenderness and sweetness in the early morning hours,
And dampness from the falling dew and the smell of summer
    showers.

The warmth of summer's intimacy hovered close and lingered still
Through autumn's russet crinkled leaves and the ice of winter's chill.

And so it was…

No strings attached, no heavy vows, no solemn oaths to fear;
The hurts and chains of yesterday are still too great, too near.

Upon this venture of two hearts the spirit must be free
To roam an unencumbered path — to move, to breathe, to be.

A hint of spring, a prelude to another summer sky
And memories of a noonday sun and the greenery of July.

And so it is…

Tommie C. Miller
*Desoto, TX*

*This was composed in the spring of 1979 under the name of Carroll Landmon.
The guy and the gal stayed together and have now been married for nearly thirty
summers. The "story behind the story" is left to the reader's imagination.*

## Seasons

Buds unravel reaching for the sun
Birds searching for twigs to build their abodes
Bees a buzzing dispensing their nectar
Spring all around, it's Mother Nature

Picnics, beach balls, swimming and fun
Skateboarding, biking
Run, run, run
Summer has arrived
A long — hot — one

Leaves change their colors: assorted hues
Squirrels search for food; anything will do
Put away the summer clothes
Bring out warm sweaters
Smell the cool midnight air
There's a new autumn weather

Overcast days, longer nights
Bring out the chill of those wintry frostbites
Light up the fireplace
Bring out the cocoa
Winter is here
We've come full circle

Theresa Romero
*Greenfield, WI*

## Cuts Like Knives

It cut deep just like a knife
Careful what you say it might end a life
Your words hurt and you don't even know
Most people just wouldn't let it show
That's why it happens, people ending their lives
It's because your words cut like knives
So keep your mouth shut before you regret it
Now you will never forget it
You ended a life with your insensitive words
You called them all names and now you just heard
They didn't want to live so they just gave in
They let you beat them but is this really a win
So watch what you say and keep your mouth shut
Because those words that you say like a knife it will cut
Ending a life you will never get back
This isn't a video game you don't get a life pack
So think before you open your trap
Or otherwise your name will get a bad wrap
Speak up but for the right reason
You might save someone's life to see another season

Karoline Marie Nelson
*Alexandria Bay, NY*

*I've used writing as an outlet for my feelings to help cope with issues I've gone through in my life. I love soccer and basketball, but writing has come easily to me. I've been published two other times for pieces I've written and I don't know where I would be without my pencil, piece of paper, and ability to write.*

## Fall

Red and golden fall the leaves
Softly to the ground.
Others hanging stubbornly
Upon the trees abound.

A canvas painted not by men
But more beautiful by far,
Are the trees in all their glory
Greeting winter from afar.

For God has made the leaves so bright
To change at His command,
From green to brown and yellow
At a gesture of His hand.

No picture made can justly show
The wonder of it all.
But God in His own master plan
Saw fit to give us fall.

Chelsea Statler
*New Providence, PA*

*I am twenty-two years old and live with my parents and three siblings. I work as a sales clerk in a local retail store. I love reading and writing and spending time with family and friends. I have been writing since I was eight years old. The inspiration for this poem came one day as I was outside reading. I looked up and was blown away by the brilliant colors of the trees. As I walked through them the words for this poem came to mind. It was my way of praising God for His handiwork. Glory be to Him!*

## Glory of the Night

How you luminate the path before
To leave but shadows on the way behind
Oh, thou glory of the night
Keeper of the stars: O light divine
Whilst you rule all be dark and still
You, O comely form, light of day do kill
Thou join the sun afore it end
And keep long after it be sent
Thine extent be great beyond thy face
For lo-by earth thy beauty placed
All yourself to earth doth lend
This stillness of night be but thy symphony penned
In your place, the sky — O, great expanse
Naught be seen, but thee in dance
At even time all life doth wait
For from day a space to take
Why wish for sun when thou O moon be here?
Ay, for with vigor I do cry: let only moon come near
My desire only for moon and I
Cast all other body out of sky
Thee, the night o'er me do keep
'Till sun doth gain
And thou, O blessed ghostly comfort
Courteously refrain

Cherith J. Wozniak
*White Cloud, MI*

## The Barn

There's something fascinating about a barn,
He sits while you pass by and bides his hours.
Will fight the snow and wind and summer showers,
And when you stop he'll listen to your yarn.

Sometimes he's like an arc that has just landed,
He welcomes the domestics and those wild,
And treats each single guest as his own child,
No notice if you're renegade or branded.

Some old ones become stores and sell antiques,
Some get makeovers when there're many leaks,
The posts, the beams, the windows people buy,
And some are left out back to wait and die.

I think of my old barn, dark, cool, secure,
The places Granddad didn't know I hid,
The mystery, fun, excitement and allure,
I'd give most anything to be a kid.

Leonardo Juan Rodriguez
*Manchester, NH*

# Her

She was a monster,
tearing me up inside to out.
She sacrificed my skin to the Goddess of
Hatred and to Death.

She was a siren,
leaving my skin raw after each attack.
She savored my blood and cursed my
feeble and fragile bones as she screeched.

She was an abyss,
swallowing me whole then spitting me out.
She laughed at my weakness in my
approach to her wicked temptations.

She was an addition,
feeding my wish to hate myself.
She told me about my worthlessness
and how I deserved to live with death.

She was my life,
my every breath, my every movement.
She ripped open my skin and left me vulnerable.
Thank God that Death didn't want us.

Autumn Geerer-Vignes
*Fort Thomas, KY*

# A New Sunset in Love

In the stillness of the evening the wind blowing through my hair
I could hear your name whispered across the sea
I closed my eyes and thanked the heavens that you were sent to me

I watched as the waves danced as they splashed in front of me how
I longed for your touch and feel your smile
I could feel your spirit from the warmth of the air as I felt the
sunset glowing a while

At times I can feel your heart beat when I feel I have lost my
way then I feel your arms around me
Walking along I see your footprints glowing in the sand and we
are walking together hand in hand the glow of Heaven is all I see

The sound of the ocean reaching out to us the waves carrying our
love within its embrace a love to last for eternity
I keep asking myself as I'm feeling the warmth of your love in my
hand your heart beats with mine that this heavenly moment was
meant to be

My eyes adored you from the moment you first looked into my eyes
your soul piercing mine with a love only Heaven could have sent
Every moment that your eyes are gazing into mine I can feel the
warmth of your loving soul with your arms around me this is how
being in love was always meant

Doug Aaron
*Phoenix, AZ*

## Stepmother

The dictionary states that she is
"the wife of one's father who is
distinct from one's natural or legal mother."

A stepmother is habitually looked at as:
the one that is considered to be evil,
the individual categorized as the blame
for many things in the family,
the family member considered as
"the extra source of income for me,"
the member that gets gossiped about the most,
the "one who is trying to replace me in my child's life."

She is none of those things,
she is actually: one-fourth of the family,
the one who has unconditional love
for a child she did not birth,
the one family member that holds
back tears and hurt feelings but
constantly remains strong to the outside world,
the one that makes purchases for the child without
the request of anyone but simply because she cares,
and lastly the member that is
actually not trying to replace anyone
but simply trying to assist in
the best way she can and forever
attempting to fit into the family
like a child that's brand new to a school.

Brandy Monique Vaughn
*Panama City, FL*

## Immortality

Through root and herb,
By faith and belief,
With science and magic,
I achieve immortality.

I laugh in Death's face,
He has no power over me.
I am my own man,
For all eternity.

"Not so fast there my boy,"
Death says with a smile.
"No one has been as foolish as you,
In oh such a while."

"You have no power over me Death,"
I say with great pride.
"Your subjects are the dead,
And I am never to die."

"That is quite true,
You never shall die,
You'll just watch everyone else.
Here is my scythe.

"I've waited so long,
For someone to make the same mistake as I,
Now you are Death,
And now I can die."

Tom Folske
*Stacy, MN*

## My Father Attended a Toga Party
## During the Blizzard of '77

He commandeth the snow to go down upon the earth
And the winter rain and the shower of his strength

Metal lunch bucket grey as the storm's forecasted birth
Held a meatloaf sandwich and licorice an arm's length

All paid jobs absorb and degrade the mind; go headfirst
Into the blizzard winds with Merry Tillers cranked

Fire departments will soon discover their dearth
But my father trekked through snow, blowing and banked

He never made it to the warehouse, for what it's worth
Traffic was stalled both ways, every lane

Rescued by a worker on a snowmobile, Firth
He was driven to the nearest hotel and stayed

And later reported the goings on: the mirth
The first night, a toga party, white sheets draped

Second night more merriment, this time a blur
A man they named Gumby got up and sang

The storm grew fiercer but to them it did not occur
That this event would trap them four more days

Barbara J. Stadler
*Lakewood, OH*

# Worst Day Ever?

Today was the absolute worst day ever
And don't try to convince me that
There's something good in every day
Because, when you take a closer look,
This world is a pretty evil place.
Even if
Some goodness does shine through once in a while
Satisfaction and happiness don't last.
And it's not true that
It's all in the mind and heart
Because
True happiness can be attained
Only if one's surroundings are good.
It's not true that good exists
I'm sure you can agree that
The reality
Creates
My attitude
It's all beyond my control
And you'll never in a million years hear me say that
Today was a very good day.

Now read it from bottom to top, the other way,
And see what I really feel about my day.

Chanie Gorkin
*Brooklyn, NY*

*Because of her talents for music and rhythm, Chanie Gorkin has always had an appreciation for poetry. She especially enjoys the works of Shel Silverstein and other poets whose styles include humor and clever twists. Chanie lives with her parents and siblings in the Chassidic community of Crown Heights, Brooklyn. Chassidic philosophy stresses that God is good, and since He is the cause of everything, everything is essentially good. Look for the good in all things and you literally create positive energy and a good reality for yourself. It all depends on how you look at it.*

## Shipwrecked by the Laughter of Gods

Redemption rolls off the tongue
pure as chlorine bleach
and at its feet lags
clean from corrupt
shackled fitful in translation

*Science without religion is lame*
*Religion without science is blind*
— I wish a wild-haired seer
had stirred sense
at my wide-eyed pulpit

and if by shared troth
I be condemned by legend of
adherence—is better than
guilt-riddled proxy.

Wanda Morrow Clevenger
*Hettick, IL*

## The Young Country Couple

As I lay here thinking I need a helping hand
One who will be with me and truly understand
To love me for me and always let me know
One to be with me and together we will grow

To understand I'm a country girl in oh so many ways
And want to live a simple life the rest of my days
To feel the warmth in his heart and together make a home
Side by side we walk the streams and together pastures roam

As I sit here thinking I need a helping hand
One that will choose me and truly understand
To want me for me and always let me know
One to stand with me wherever we will go

To understand I'm a country boy through and through
Together live a simple life doing things we do
To know her touch as we walk hand in hand
Knowing I have the one I want and together walk the land

Paul Morris
*Tuscumbia, AL*

## Trapped in Illusions

Again and again I feel like I'm robbed of my happiness.
I did all I could do to deny that the glass had tipped.
I have a lot of good in me
but these demons they won't let me be
won't let the light shine through.
Innocence trapped in a lonely hue.
Feeling lost, afraid and hopeless
history shows that this is disaster's cue.
So I scream for repentance not your attention
stop treating me less than you.
I wish I could wish, with my soul I would kiss
with my luck I would miss.
Stuck in a spiral, temptation is viral and the "want" that we "need"
it seems vital.
In a world so seduced by society
it's important for people to walk right beside of me.
I walk to insanity praying the heavens will come grab a hold of me.
Until that time comes take my hand
helping me help you keep our feet on the ground.
You have to get lost, before you get found.

Bradley Mckay Luke
*Bellingham, WA*

*I'm currently twenty-one years old and I've lived in Bellingham, WA, my whole
life. When I wrote this poem I was at the lowest point in my life: dealing with my
three-month-old son's death in 2012, fighting a battle against CPS for custody
of my newborn daughter, struggling with a vicious drug and alcohol addiction,
homeless and in a relationship with a very violent man. Putting my thoughts and
emotions onto paper was the only real release I had left.*

# Home for the Holidays

Trees filling houses with bright neon lights
Stockings are hung on the mantles and walls
Children wait eagerly, counting the nights
Families are quickly decking the halls

Songs on the radio bring us much joy
Kids racing down snowy hills in their sleigh
Presents are filled with every type of toy
Finally we make it to Christmas day

Wrapping paper covers living room floors
Later tonight we will have a big party
Relatives are knocking on the doors
We sit down to eat meals that are hearty

Outside Jack Frost tries to nip at our nose
Inside we try to warm up our toes

Amber Lansford
*Jasper, IN*

## Man

A man stands tall and his mind is taller.
His imagination reaches beyond the stars.
He walks on two feet and calls himself king.
He kills wildlife without a thought.
He builds mountains that reach the sky.
What he loves, he takes care of, what he hates he destroys.
Future generations will come as before.
There must be room beyond the star's door.
Now I ask you my friend, Is this the *supreme being?*
So the next time you do, think twice before  doing.
The whole Universe depends on you and you depend on the
Universe.

Robert Geiersbach

*I was nineteen years old in high school when I wrote this poem. I started running trains at age twenty under supervision of regular engineers. At age twenty-three, I became a certified locomotive engineer and worked for thirty-five years. I worked for Penn Central, Conrail, Grand Trunk and Canada National railroads. My dad worked for Michigan Central and New York Central railroads. The most important thing I have learned in life, from Psalm 7:8: it is important for a person to develop integrity.*

# Untitled

A crisp December night shown off in festive light
I awoke without warning to a white winter morning
A blanket of snow upon the ground
Had fallen, without a sound
It made me wonder hard and long
Where had my friend the summer gone?
He slipped away when I wasn't looking
After the hamburgers were done cooking
He took the birds, the warm breeze
Even the shade beneath our trees
He took the sun upon my face
And left a chill in its place
I should have thanked him everyday
Maybe then he would have stayed
As I lament over summer's haste
I feel it all may be a waste
For the change of season like a call to duty
On a winter's morn is so full of beauty!

Randy Roberts
*Cameron Park, CA*

## Tekken's Mark

Sometimes when I close my eyes I see you on my lap kissing my face
or just sitting watching TV.
It's strange now I realize how much my life you were a part of,
I hope I repaid you for your loyalty and love,
with the best life you could dream of.
I keep you in my heart with all my memories of fifteen years:
the good times, bad times and tears.
You've touched me down to the depths of my soul;
that kind of connection I'm afraid I will never again know.
The thought of even trying would mean my feelings I'm denying.
I would not even be able to compare
nor there be any competition because it's you I am longing for
and missing,
though it's wonderful to have the memories for reminiscing.
Blessed that I felt that kind of emotion,
to give unconditionally and wholeheartedly with such devotion.
Some of it is a natural trait of the breed.
What is it? You ask, an American pit bull terrier indeed.
Though right now we can't be together,
we will meet someday again, my beloved friend,
at the gates of Heaven.

Hope M. Larrimore
*Lehighton, PA*

# Trio

My trio of sons: two blonds and a dark-haired curly top
United against your mother in the pursuit of mischief
Decorating walls and furniture
Mutilating toys
Digging to China with a rubber hose and a stream of crystal
Building contraptions of scraps and a thousand nails!

And the flip side —
Digging for hours and tramping through brush to build me a
  wild garden in the yard
Bringing wild rose bushes from the swamp 'cause you love me
Helping in my day care
  playing with kids who weren't related
  except through love bonds
Fetching the nails, the tools and extension cords
  helping your dad build things of red and gold
Then working in popcorn wagons standing on milk boxes
  burning your hands
Teasing your sisters or picking on your little brother
Oh, how they'll miss it!
Unspoken losses, but felt nonetheless, as you head off
  to college
My trio of sons

May God bless and keep you!

Mary Rohr
*Bertha, MN*

# The Final Statement

After the excuses
how they insidiously mount
the challenges and tribulations
we all must surmount
it matters not
where or how we began
or whether a great talent
heeded our command
The final statement
we speak ourselves
what we valued
our lives do tell

Some will create beauty
out of dirt and decay
while others will let paradise
slip away

Madeline Drake
*Los Angeles, CA*

*Madeline Drake is a writer and award winning poet living in Los Angeles, California. The poem, "The Final Statement," is the concluding poem in her book,* The Mirror of Perfect Reflection, *which is a spiritual journey, told through poetry. In addition to poetry, Madeline has written screenplays and children's books and is currently working on independently producing her romantic comedy screenplay,* Soul Mates. *Madeline has worked as a copywriter and TV commercial producer in NYC and has produced situation comedy in Los Angeles. Ms. Drake is currently preparing* The Mirror of Perfect Reflection *for a 2015 publication.*

## Secret Love in the Past

Our love is clearly in the past
It was all good while it did last

These memories I'll secretly hold inside
To no one will I confide

Maybe as time marches on
I'll write about it in a song

Bernadette Bonacci
*Philadelphia, PA*

## Diplomacy

I would cease all killing if I could
    But can I when you kill?

I would wipe out all hunger if I could
    But can I feed all you starve?

Peace is balance like a two-sided coin
    Standing on its end

I shall balance the coin
    Will you balance it too?

Mary Miller
*Belvidere, IL*

# Finally — The Light

I kept hustlin' — I kept grindin'
On my way to the top, yet I'm still climbin'
And when I think about the days before
I put a smile on my face and say thank you to the Lord
For all that I have, all the blessings in my life
Like my wonderful son and oh, so beautiful wife
A family who loves me and wants me to succeed
They provide the support and caring words that I need
There was a time in my past when anger filled all my veins
Then I opened my eyes, looked towards the sky
Saw that mountaintop and continued to climb

Now I sit in this place, this place of anger and shame
This prison of hatred, I put myself in this game
The choices I made, I've got no one to blame
Except for myself for all of this pain
All this time to think, all this time to talk
It's time to ask for help and choose what path to walk
It's time to ask for forgiveness for all of my sins
Without the Lord in my life, I truly cannot win
Now I'm doing my best to live a good life
With his glory and grace it will be worth the price
That I'll have to pay, but at the end of the day
I'll look towards the sky and I'll continue to pray

Colby Rohan
*Tolland, CT*

# Never Again

The edges of the article are tattered, yellow and torn
The people in it had their arms numbered and their heads shorn.
They were shipped by rail to a living hell.

They were ripped from their homes
No longer their own.
They were no longer allowed to take a fresh breath
Only allowed to smell the stench of death.

Their homes had names that were meant to sound auspicious
But in reality they were Bergen-Belsen, TreBlinka, and Auschwitz.

When the gates were opened in 1945
Once again you could see hope and faith in their eyes.
We as a society must make sure that an atrocity like this never
happens again.
Thank you. Amen.

Glenn A. Powell
*Winchester, KY*

## The Lighthouse

When I travel by train, bus, airplane I always see them.
When I visit New York or New Jersey I always see them.
When I visit Boston and the Northern Atlantic sea coast I always
  see them.
When I visit Canada the Pacific Ocean side I always see them.
When I visit Alaska I always see them.
When I visit Oregon and Washington State I always see them.
When I visit California's Pacific Coast I always see them.
When I visit Mexico's Gulf Coast I always see them.
When I visit Mississippi and Alabama I always see them.
When I visit New Orleans I always see them.
When I visit Florida I always see them.
When I visit Georgia I always see them.
When I visit South Carolina I always see them.
When I visit North Carolina I always see them.
When I visit Lake Ontario I always see them.
When I visit Lake Erie I always see them.
When I visit Lake Superior I always see them.
When I visit Lake Huron I always see them.
When I visit Lake Michigan I always see them.
When I visit Hawaii I always see them.
When I visit Sicily, Italy, I always see them.
When I visit Nicosia, Cyprus, I always see them.
When I am walking I always see them.
When I am driving my car I always see them.
I always have wondered do those lighthouses ever see me?

John Nicosia
*Arlington Heights, IL*

# Our Farm Today

Cornfield, pasture,
hill, dale and hollow:
just as they were.

But only the windmill
  remains standing.

Its rust covered frame
  a skeleton obelisk;

Its creaking tin blade still
  flying on high.

Each passing breeze eliciting
  a mournful dirge to a
  graveyard of self interred
  outbuildings.

Each plot and tomb marked with
  a disheveled mausoleum of
  broken beam, plank and
  shingle.

Barn machine shed, hog house,
  hen house and milk house:
  lie asunder on the sod.

Roof and foundation of
  each resting structure
  locked in eternal
  embrace.

Doug Herron
*Wood Dale, IL*

*These lines were penned while viewing the desolation of an abandoned Iowa farmstead that once belonged to my great uncle. Only the landscape and bountiful crops were as I had remembered them.*

## Little Boy Lost

Little boy why do you cry,
Is it because you're hungry, and don't know why.
In your sadness there's no one to really care,
No one around you has anything that they can really spare.
It's been so long since you've had any shoes,
This isn't the life you would care to choose.
Your mother died from a disease you couldn't spell,
The emptiness grows but there's no one to tell.
Sometimes you're thirsty, your throat so dry,
Nothing safe to drink, you don't dare try.
Often at nights you're alone, and so very cold.
Your family's all gone, or so you've been told.
Lots of times, you feel depressed, and all alone,
So far removed from the only life you've ever known.

Louis Graziaplena
*Belle Isle, FL*

# Relative

A minute
seems longer
than any hour
I've
ever
crossed
but that's relative;
in the great scheme
of orbiting bodies
time means nothing
like the patter of rain
means nothing
to the fiery sun
and the suffering
of a voiceless, screaming
child
means nothing
to the listening deafness
of our superiors
and yet
we still ask ourselves:
what could possibly
be going
so terribly
absolutely
wrong?

Kortnie Wheaton
*Attleboro, MA*

# A Broken-Hearted Lover

When you and I first met
I trusted you from the start.
You lied, cheated, sneaked,
And then you broke my heart.

Now since I found you out,
It will never be the same.
You never meant to be true.
You were out to play a game.

I have met crooks before, but
From you this I did not expect.
My life is not the same, and
My heart is a wreck.

Someday I'll get over this.
A lesson I have learned:
To make sure I know I'm truly loved
Before I give my heart to anyone.

Geraldine Pope
*Cocoa, FL*

# More

Another book to be read,
Another idea to fill your head.
More words yet to be spoken,
More promises to be broken.
More peace to be made,
Another debt to be paid.
Another war to be won,
Another day gone and done.
Another plea to demand,
Another problem to understand.
Another place to be seen,
Another yes, no, or maybe.
Another true love another heartbreak,
Another thing you want and take.
Another question, another date,
Another thing to love or hate.
More time to be spent
Another bill! Must pay the rent!
More places you dare not go,
More people to meet, friend or foe.
Another thing you must do,
Another second you are you.
Another job you have done,
More time to have some fun.
Trips, journeys, adventures galore,
No matter how much you do, there's so much more!

Shayna Alexis Mango
*Norfolk, MA*

*Hi, my name is Shayna Mango! I wrote this poem in 2014 at age eleven. I got the idea for this poem from a case of writer's block. Actually, it was more like a case of writer's flood. Ideas were flowing in from every direction, and I simply couldn't choose which to write about. "It's no use!" I had thought, "no matter what, there is always so much more!" And that's how I got the punch line, and title, for my poem. It's an honor to be published in this book, and to get to share my inspiration with you.*

# The Calico Hunter

Stalking through the tall grass
the haze of dusk upon the sky
her sights set upon the bird
as it continues to fly

There is a branch low hanging
for which the bird takes a break
the calico spots this
it's her move to make

Locked deep in her stare
in a crouch she spies her prey
she rocks back and makes her move
this lucky bird flies away

The target was a bit too fast
her instinct proved to be right
as she ponders what could have been
she'll have to wait for the next flight

Mark Katz
*Martinez, CA*

# Untitled

The years growing up
As I look back and think
We really had it all including
"The kitchen sink!"

Mom and Dad to show us
Live right, have fun!
All the weekends at Lake Benedict
Under that bright, shiny sun!

The house we grew up in,
Neighborhood friends to play ball
Now seems like a mansion, Mom always said,
*"This @#*% kitchen's too small."*

The family gatherings of both sides,
In awe of the memories!
Love thick in the air
Two big, happy families!

Three-son headache for Mom
Three-son pride for Dad
One thing for sure
They gave us everything they had!

So much more to say,
But time being the issue.
Besides that… I really need a tissue!

We love and thank you
Mom and Dad.

Tom Klopstein
*Racine, WI*

# The Party Girl

Put on your best dress,
You gotta look great.
'Cause we're going to party,
Till late, late, late.

Dancing and drinking
We're going to feel fine,
Laughing and kissing
Havin' the best ol' time.

Year after year,
I think the last one's best,
But found out this year,
Is better than the rest.

When this party's over,
It's one day at a time.
You as my "party girl"
Everything's just fine.

Happy birthday, happy birthday
I hope you have a great time.
'Cause when the last guest leaves,
You'll be all mine.
Hmm!

I love you always,
Your adoring husband,
Ed, Whiz, Big Bear.

Ed Whisenant
*Mansfield, TX*

*Known as Whiz by friends and associates, I grew up in Texas and Oklahoma. This poem is about my wife on her fifty-eighth birthday after twenty-three years of marriage. I give her poetry several times a year, and have for many years, for events such as birthdays, Valentine's, anniversaries, and so on. She is my inspiration to write and poetry gives me an avenue to express my love and affection for her. I hope to write several more over the years celebrating our love.*

## Wheel of Fortune

Dear Pat and Vanna,

Just a note to set you straight.
Some letters are vowels and some letters ain't.
"A-E-I-O-U" is the vowel cry,
But don't forget "and sometimes Y."

A-Y and O-Y, Y works with a vowel that's near.
Put Y on the end for a vowel you can hear.
Baby and cry, vowel Y on the end;
Yellow and yes, consonant Y to begin.

Guarding the wheel and turning each letter,
Planning new puzzles, you make the game better.
Pat and Vanna, you really are great,
But K is a consonant, Y always ain't!

Jean Olson
*Elk Grove, CA*

*As a reading specialist teacher, I believed in a strong phonics-based program. In the audience of an early taping of the "Wheel of Fortune" show this bit of whimsy came to mind. I sent a copy in 1990 to the studio and received a picture postcard with "Thanks for the vowel lesson," but alas! they are still calling "Y" a consonant!*

## A Mother's Love for Her Sons

They begin so helpless and so small
A mother does everything for them from simple tasks to all.
She takes care of their basic needs
It just comes from love and her many deeds.
Memories once cherished with each milestone
She dreads the day when she'll be all alone.
They begin to become independent
She wonders where all the time went.
Sports and play dates fill the days
They're becoming men in so many ways.
Dating, prom, and graduation
College around the corner will be a new addition
Then one gets married and takes a wife
Now he has his own life.
Can grandchildren be far away?
Her love will grow on that glorious day!

Sandy Erickson
*Hibbing, MN*

*My name is Sandy Erickson. I have two boys ages twenty-four and twenty-one. I also have a new daughter-in-law as of December 27, 2013. My younger son, Steven, has been dating a wonderful girl for four-plus years. I love all these young adults very much. Thinking of all the love that I have for my children inspired me to write this poem. I have been a single parent since my boys were six and nine years old. I have worked hard to bring up responsible and respectable young men. I look forward to what the future will bring for our family.*

# I Am…

I am intelligent and kind.
I refuse to fight for revenge.
I want world peace.
I am intelligent and kind.

I am intelligent and kind.
I think of those who weep.
I worry I might fail.
I am intelligent and kind.

I am intelligent and kind.
I believe all will be good.
I hope for day and not night.
I am intelligent and kind.

Christopher Gibson
*Pine Bush, NY*

# I'm So Lost in You

Upon thinking of you, I lose track of everything that's all around me.
I even lose track of everything that's affiliated with time.
Why?
Simply because of who you are, and the way that you consume my
mind, and when I look at you, all I can think about is you because
I'm so lost in you.
I'm engrossed by your beauty, and I fail not to love and protect
you, because that's my duty.
You see I'm so lost in you, and I choose to be with you, even when
you're sometimes moody.
I'm so lost in you, and I'm so into you, just like the sun, moon, and
stars are into the sky that's so high above.
I can't give you everything, but I can and will give you all of my love.

Artis Trawick
*Fitzgerald, GA*

*Hello everyone, my name is Artis Trawick. I've been writing since I was fourteen years old. To me writing is therapy. I love it! In 2008, I received the Editor's Choice Award certificate for a poem that I wrote to the International Library of Poetry. The poem is entitled "Forever Mine." It's already published, you will find it in a book called* The Sound of Poetry. *I have so much to tell you and not enough space. May God's blessings be upon you always.*

# Untitled

There once was a boy
Who would cry everyday
It's because he didn't have any friends
He couldn't live that way
His class made fun of him
Which made him feel sad
His class bullied him
And it made him feel bad
He goes home,
Then his mom said, "What's wrong?"
"Nothing," he said,
"This is where I don't belong"
Back at school,
Getting bullied again
He has choices in mind
But he doesn't know where to begin
Again at home,
His mom said, "What's wrong with you?"
He said, "I'm getting bullied,
I don't know what to do"
His mom said, "Okay
Well let's just pray
Hopefully tomorrow
Will be a better day"

Gavin Hirn
*Jacksonville, NC*

## Family Reunion

We lie on the bed, my cousin and I,
Giggling in the dark.
We peek through the screen
At a navy sky,
Breathing in damp nippy air.
The yellow glow from the room down the hall
Bears the gentle voices of those we know.
The scent of homemade soap,
The sheets tucked tight on the bed,
The soft old quilt pulled up to our ears,
Wrap us in Grandma's calm cocoon.
Our little fingers pledge "friends forever"
Before we sleep the sleep of children
Loved.

Linda E. Evans
*Huntsville, TX*

*This poem reflects days of childhood when my grandparents ran a working farm with pigs, cows, chickens, horses, a collie, a barn, mice and cats in Missouri. I had eight aunts and uncles and twenty-plus cousins, which made going to Grandma's a truly special time. Because Daddy had moved us to Texas, part of the fun for us kids was the travel itself to and from Missouri: eating at restaurants, making "pit stops," singing folk songs, and gas stops when we occasionally bought snacks. We often traveled for Thanksgiving and Christmas and occasionally through the summer when we had big picnics at the park. A bonus was to travel also to my mama's family in Northern Missouri. As I have become a mother and grandmother myself, I appreciate that my parents taught me the importance of family, even if it takes hard work to maintain.*

# The Star of the Show

Some people stand on center stage
And enjoy applause of men.
And when the spotlight's beam is on
Want it to shine on them.

But have you ever wondered
About the work that's done
Before the curtain opens
And the plot begins to run?

For somewhere in the shadows,
Often out of view,
Is someone doing those thankless tasks
That no one else would do.

Without these humble heroes
The show would not go on.
There would be no opening curtain —
There would be no opening song.

Yet each day the "play" continues.
Each night a star is born.
While some enjoy the limelight,
Anonymously some perform.

Some names appear on marquee lights.
Some names we never know.
But one without the other
Would quickly stop the show.

Darwin W. Gough
*Keyser, WV*

# Bill Collectors

Bill collectors, bill collectors
They keep knocking at my door.
They're at the windows
On the rooftops
And they're coming through the floor!

Bill collectors, bill collectors
Go away and leave me be
For I'm slowly going crazy
Getting up the dough for thee.

When I've paid you,
And I've made you,
Just as happy as can be,
I'll be resting
Nice and easy,
I'll be dead and gone you see!

Robert C. Rann
*Sierra Madre, CA*

*My dearest dad wrote the above ditty. He sang it to us using the melody of "Oh My Darling Clementine." Dad wrote other poems and created other works, but unfortunately, only a few remain. Although Dad was a great poet and writer, he was never published. It was my heart's desire to see my dad published one day, so I am very pleased to have Eber & Wein publish his poem. My father passed away at the age of forty-nine in 1967. He is, and has always been, my greatest inspiration in life.*

# Journey

Let me take you on a journey,
   Where dawn breaks, into a palette of color.

Where the air is fragrant with flowers.
   And the weeping willow wakes to the morning sun.

Birds singing their songs, within the
   branches, thank you!  A new day has begun.

The creek, is melody to my heart, as it
   ripples across its shiny rocks ladened with fish.

Beckoning wildlife, I see a coyote in the
   distance, drink without fear, water crystal clear.

Surrounded by mountains, red and tall
   covered with fir trees waiting for Christmas
   Like sentinels guarding intruders.

My mind far removed, from city noise
   cars, with honking sounds and humans
   intoxicated loud and rude.

"Sedona," I ache for you.  I yearn to stroll in
   Your majestic splendor.  To nourish
   every inch of my being.

The noise of the city continues
   from dawn to dusk, only to bring
   me back to you.  For you are deep in my heart.

Anna Kowsky
*Palm Desert, CA*

# My Father

You are morning
To my night.
The sun
To my moon.
When life gets darkest,
You are the light.

An ear
To my voice.
A smile
To my frown.
Understanding
My life, my choices.

Life goes on,
Our situations change.
You are my constant.
My father,
Always remains.

Donna M. Wheelehon
*Las Vegas, NV*

# Tragedy in New York:
# Destruction of the Twin Towers

On September 11, 2001,
I was sitting in my office all alone.
Awaiting the beginning of a brand new day
(As I normally do) I began to pray.

All at once, I heard a loud crash!
The building shook! I made a mad dash!
I joined many others who tried to leave.
We prayed, as we fled, for last minute reprieve!
It was not God's plan for me to be spared.
This moment of doom, with many, was shared.

God's angels were with us in our despair.
They lifted our souls right out of the air,
And bore them on to our resting place
Until we meet Jesus face to face!

May God bless those
We left behind
And replace their grief
With love for mankind.

Marianne Donahoe
*Jackson, MS*

*On the morning of September 11, 2001, my daughter called from her office in New Jersey, across the river from the Twin Tower buildings. Her voice was trembling when she said, "Mother... a plane just hit one of the Twin Towers!" Then... "Oh... another plane just hit! People are jumping from windows! Turn your television on!" As I watched this disaster unfold on television, I imagined I was in the building. I wondered how God could comfort the people experiencing this tragedy. As I prayed, God sent an answer... He sent His angels!*

## Angel in White

Holding her lamp...
with its ethereal light.

Aiding the sick...
by day and by night.

A woman of patience...
and courage is she.

All clothed in white...
a symbol of purity.

The cap on her...
shiny head of brown.

Symbolizing that...
of an angel's crown.

God made thee...
to love and to care.

Assisting the needy...
in time of despair.

What e'er the time...
be it day or night.

You will find...
this *angel in white*.

All over the land...
in our hospitals tonight.

Doris J. Mawn
*Riverside, CA*

## Shangri-La

The blue sky and vast ocean on horizon meet,
Endless waves over sandy beach splash my feet.
Peace and tranquility fill the air,
Gentle breezes caress my hair.
Here *Shangri-La* you've ben waiting for me,
A restful haven may it forever be.
You nourish my heart and my soul,
You enrich my life, you make me whole.
Though I journey on and cannot stay,
We will meet again soon, for that I pray.

Frank Scibior
*San Carlos, CA*

## The Sea of Forget

I saw a crystal river outside the throne of God.
It is a glass-like substance that held the sins of all.
He stands upon its shoreline to throw the sins all in.
It's the Sea of Forget that I will never forget.

Precious is each drop of blood that paid the price
so that all my sins would find their way into its glassy ice.
Cold and dark are the depths where each sin lies.
It is the Sea of Forget that I will never forget.

Crystal M. Davis
*Litchfield, IL*

## Tell Me Where Is My World

Tell me where is my world.
Aurora, Newtown, Ferguson — healing is coming.
Tell me where is my world.
Trayvon Martin, Hadiya Pendleton, Michael Brown — we miss you.
Tell me where is my world.
Columbine, Virginia Tech, Sandy Hook — continue to be survivors.
Tell me where is my world because it does not belong here.
The murdered, the bullied and the abused.
I am among them so I know the feeling.
I am the descendent of slaves, I am among them, yet, I walk
   alongside demons.
Tell me where is my world.

Tell me where is my world. It does not belong in this war.
A war where the innocent are taken every day and every night.
A war where even small children are being killed.
A war of guns, blood and disharmony.
Tell me where is my world, because it does not belong here.
I tried to let things be — thinking that the world would get better.
But I am done standing in the silence.  My cries of mercy are not
   being heard.
Tell me where is my world.
Being silent will no longer stand with this injustice that we live in.
Tell me where is my world.
Someone please tell me where is my world…

LaKesia D. Session
*Sumter, SC*

# The Last Questions

Peach pink skies, peeping through slatted blinds,
The newborn light resting on my quiet body
As my mind worries over the whirling vortex of a waning world.
Knowing the end is near,
I wonder whether I should die in defiant action
Or remain in dignified stillness.
Too late for the former.
I look again at the window
And adjust my head, inside and out.
To see the pastel skies slowly turn to purple black.
I am not sorry for the destruction of man —
He has done this to himself.
But I mourn the planet's loss of living creatures,
Innocent of hate and greed.
From jungles, mountains, plains and fields
And all the waterways which gave us life
Will complete destruction give this world a new beginning?
And will I be born again?

Gloria Rasmussen
*Fort Myers, FL*

# True Love

If you can overlook someone's faults
and forgive without regret,

If you can forgive their biting words,
which mean no harm,

If you can feel the bitter pain
of the other's suffering,

If you can sing with joy
when the other is ecstatic,

If there is no morsel to share,
and you gladly give them yours,

To see perfection, when there are so many flaws.

To give up your life, so the other may live,

To give of yourself, with no reservations,

To know all these things,
is to open a small space inside your heart,
to let you know what true love is.

Genevieve Vascimini
*Whiting, NJ*

# Undying Love

The love of my life need not be so handsome that
He would turn someone's head
But only with him would I give my true love
And share my bed
The man of my heart should only be one
Until my life on earth is done
It would be my joy to bring him pleasure
His smile is worth more than any treasure
On his chest my chest does lay
Our beating hearts with each other play
After we have shared each other in our most intimate way
Laying in his arms is how I long to end my day
Sometimes in the middle of the night
I'd awake to find him in a dream so deep
And I thank my God for my loved one
That lies beside me in sweet sleep

Matthew J. Hammer
*Tucson, AZ*

*This was a eulogy I wrote for a grieving wife and mother because she felt guilty for not being present at her handicapped husband's bedside when he passed. These are the last words she would have said face to face when he was still alive. After she read the poem, there was not a dry eye at the funeral service.*

## War and My Life

In the year nineteen-forty-five
in the month of June I came alive.
The world was sure the war was done
all America was grateful we had won.
Men had suffered and many had died
women mourned and all had cried.
This was the end of a horrific war
people rejoiced and their hearts did soar.
I started school at the age of six
not really knowing of the Korean mix.
Again men fought and many men died
in nineteen-fifty-three the war would subside.
Through most of my schooling things were cool
then in the end I was but a fool.
Vietnam had become more than a thought
because this new draft had got men caught.
I joined the Navy and loved the sea
I guess others decided to flee.
I served four years and was proud of every bit
shortly thereafter would be the end of it.
Most people search for peace of mind
isn't it ironic how much war we find.
It's now two-thousand-and-fourteen
from war to war with so little time between.
I'm going to end this just in time
shouldn't war really be a worldwide crime?

Vernon R. Moyer
*Vancouver, WA*

# Little Yellow Butterfly

Little yellow butterfly
Again I see you
Flutter by
Sometimes more than a moment
You capture my eye
As I gaze in awe
I think it's you Cindy
Our angel, beautiful butterfly.
Dad says you may be watching over him
He sees you as he cuts the grass.
Sometimes in my car
I see you fly on past my windshield glass
Home from work
You greet me near the front door
Oh Cindy, how I long everyday to see you more.
When you fly away suddenly
I get sad and sigh
I never want to say "good-bye."
I think often how you adored butterflies in life
What a tribute to who you were
Beautiful, independent, and free
Everytime I see "our little yellow butterfly"
I think of you
And how much you will always mean to me.

Colleen Graham
*Port St. Lucie, FL*

*The inspiration for my poem was the tragic loss of my sister, Cindy. Cindy was taken from our family on Thanksgiving Day unexpectedly. Writing was very therapeutic for me to help me deal with her loss and express my grief. I looked for signs of comfort and I noticed often a little yellow butterfly around me. My father noticed a yellow butterfly around him as well. I believe Cindy is my "little yellow butterfly" and hope this poem inspires anyone who has lost someone to always know they're never alone. Our angels are "among us always."*

## Isolated

I never new thin glass could be so thick
Till, I am held behind it
Sad and alone the feelings are all the same,
Way too familiar.
I know it happens everyday,
People are sad, depressed, people get mad
But it is all the same, hid from the world.
In my own world alone, is where everyone is destined to be.

Anna Raquel Vallas
*Arlington, TX*

## Writing

Writing is like a stream flowing with imagination,
the moving pencil writing steadily.
I see a writer thinking of the journey of imagination.
She likes to travel to places and worlds,
meeting people that aren't really there.
Challenges come but she pushes through.
She gets stuck but that doesn't stop her.
She looks at the page, proud of herself.
Smiling, she sighs with relief.
Weight off her shoulders.
She reads it to herself and thinks of the journey made for her.

Juliet Latta
*San Anselmo, CA*

# Learning to Live Alone

Awake in the morning
To the emptiness of heart
There's no warm feeling
Another human body imparts.

The abruptness of a new day
Without Wimpy's presence
Tears into my consciousness
Like a knife into feathers.

But, my foot touches something
And there is Sox!
My puppy, warm and ready to snuggle
A reason for me to smile and cuddle.

Now fully in tune
As a new day begins
I listen for Fenway,
My kitten, and other friend.

So let the sun shine in
Face the day with a grin
Up and out to walk and
Feed my friends.

There are clothes to wash
Food to cook
Lists to check
A new day to live.

Thanks be to God.

Jeanne O. Barbour
*Chapel Hill, NC*

# What If

What if you woke up today
Only to see a child play;

What if that child called your name
And you thought he was insane;

What if hot turned to cold
Would that actually stop
The mold
Forming on your lips;

What if you became a little miffed
At someone screaming
What if;

What if your parents had named you
What If?

Evelyn Beeman
*Ashtabula, OH*

## Peace. Shoot. Gone.

She always put two fingers in the air to say good-bye.
Though, this time, it's too bad that her two fingers are together,
and her thumb is out wide.
She pressed it to her temple,
still saying good-bye,
but this time it's forever.

Alexa Pecorelli
*Canton, OH*

## When

I didn't know the breath of it.
Staring into a deep black room.
Where the flood of people
Left a dying cold
I stood and waited for my
Love to come, in the innocence
Of her white laced fury.
I do — now

Jack Ripka
*Whitestone, NY*

*June 2, 1962, I stood alone in a daze staring out into a very large, dark, rectangular room. To my left, running the length of the room, was a shear backlit curtain. Slowly, I saw her shadow walking the length of it. Suddenly she was there in the full light of the entranceway. She approached. We said the words, I do — I do. I stomped down hard and broke the glass. It was consummated.*

## Spring

The welcome sun warms the hungry earth
And prepares it for its needs.
Soon springtime flowers will blossom forth
From long dormant, sleeping seeds.

The gentle breezes, so soft and cool,
Stir the branches of the trees.
Birds fly in among the leaves
And hover there with grace and ease.

'Tis the season of cloud-filled skies,
When dreams seem to come true.
When winter's long, cold time is gone
And skies are bright and blue.

To enjoy this magical time of year
One need not have a reason.
So, welcome fragrant, vibrant spring,
The year's most lovely season.

Wanda Young
*Fontana, CA*

## To an Unborn Baby

God call you early because he needed
an angel in heaven.
Although we know you are in a better
Place  Mommy and daddy still missing you.
Be happy there baby while I am thinking
on you every minute of my life.
You left without knowing the world
the world that waited for you too.
But you never came home.
I love you so much that I feel
You are all the beauty around me.
But some day finally I am going be at
the end of my road, and we going be
together for ever.

Rebecca Deciga
*Ft. Lupton, CO*

# I Saw My Mother Cry

At an early age in my life, I caught my mother by surprise.
And at that moment of surprise, I saw teardrops in her eyes.

I saw my mother cry but I never could understand why.
"Is it a fault of mine," I asked, "the reason why you cry?"

She did not say a word but gave me her customary look,
telling me that I was just a child and would not understand.

I saw my mother cry and I know she cried for love,
as she cried in silence, to conceal her aching heart.

I saw my mother cry and I will never forget that day,
knowing that she had to keep her aching heart all to herself.

I saw my mother cry.

Edelmiro J. Villareal
*Edinburg, TX*

## Ars Poetica

A poem is sometime
Sort of thing…
Needing to be written…
Sometime…
Poems are waiting
To be released
From the dead burden of the
Merely possible…
Of only longing to be said… or heard…
Or put like this upon a page.
They are waiting to be a new…
And fresh…
And finely as well as finally
Crafted and read
Or said
Expansion of the
Meaning of the world
In the word…
Sometime…

Graham Hutchins
*Port Angeles, WA*

*In a book of seven poems,* Some Words for All Seasons, *I wrote the first poem "Some Seasoned Words" last as a summary and anticipation of the others, so here in "Ars Poetica" I seek to address the task of poetry as a preface to the works of doing it. I have enjoyed a rich career in university teaching in philosophy and humanities and have served as a clergyman on five continents. An anthology of my writings,* Paper Trails, *is now developing a second volume.* Some Words for All Seasons *is now published with my photographs.*

## Louve

Snow falls across the land I own
Lift my head up towards the sky
Imagine I could fly to the moon
My gold eyes shining triumphantly
But I was born with strong legs
Not a pair of strong wings
So I will run and I will run
And I will always be free
Through snow, rain, wind, and heat
I lead my family on and on
With grace and mystique
I am a guide, a teacher, and I
Will never die, I am strong
Gaze upon my face, find my eyes,
Through them I see your soul, your hopes,
Your dreams, and I will help
To start you on the right path
For I am wise and I am wild
Let me show you the beauty
Of wildness that lives in everyone
I am a she-wolf
I am the *louve*

Paige Lauren Dillard
*Lakeside, CA*

## Sunrise

Sitting at my table, coffee cup in my hand.
I was not feeling all that grand,
Looking out the window at the black sky.
"It is just one of those days." I sighed.
And the sun began to chase the gloom away.
It was the beginning of a beautiful day.
Once more God was painting the sky so bright,
A vision that filled me with delight.
It seemed like an answer to my prayer,
For God's love seemed to be everywhere.
If only the whole world could see,
How wonderful this life could be.
The black old gloom would go away.
God's love would brighten every day.

Elsie K. Burnette
*Leitchfield, KY*

# A Fawning Meadow

Foreshadowing any doubts of which to cope,
My memory envisions a time of hope. Dawning
On me, at the break of day, is a meadow of
Baby fawns beginning to play.

Silhouettes of childlike images, makes a past
Time of treasures a crop to cream. Stories
About a wonderful, magnificent dove, brings
A lifetime of visions sent from above.

The best time of growth, in planting a seed,
Is when happiness transpires to those we need.
A rare commodity instills in me, a beautiful
Rainbow filled with glee. Now is the time for
Us to share, about bringing sunshine and
Smiles to those we love.

Pertaining to a cause that becomes the norm,
To become a champ, we must muscle our way
To form a method of conditioning, creating
In us a structuring of sorts, strengthening
Our desire to come alive, we must jive talk
And sway to a beautiful day.

When developing a notion to become a writer,
Poetry makes a person feel brighter. With
A cheerful disposition of a meaningful
Existence, a life of leisure should be measured
Into a moment in time that should be treasured.

Anna Marie Carlson
*Port Angeles, WA*

# Good-Bye Summer

The bright harvest moon shines its golden glow,
On the Kootenai River far below.

Northwest Montana is beginning to see,
The change in the weather upon every tree.

The birch and the aspen leaves gold and brown
Flutter in the breeze as they tumble to the ground.

Soon the larch, on the mountains, will turn a bright yellow,
As the hunters wait for the elk to bellow.

Fall comes every year with the geese flying south,
Squirrels scampering up trees with winter food in their mouth.

Good-bye long summer days with warmth beyond measure,
Hello cooler weather… the seasons I'll treasure.

Connie Frederick
*Troy, MT*

## A Bookmark

Until I am ready for the war to continue
A bookmark stands between the battles.

It places a flower at the end of a quarrel,
And when I read again, the friends will be lovers.

It stands between songs I want to learn
From the songbook on the piano.

It argues no opinions, but moves graciously
From and to the places I choose.

A bookmark demands no haste
As it holds a place,
　　　　Awaiting my beach or bower
　　　　Or just someplace comfy.

All  by itself
　　　　It reminds me of the friend who tucked it
Into a book of his choosing,
　　　　Believing I would love the book.

The book, long ago read, sits somewhere
　　　　While I move the bookmark
　　　　　　From battles to lovers,

　　　　Always remembering my friend.

Rosemary Watts
*College Place, WA*

# Flaunt It

The competition is next week,
Don't be nervous do not freak.
Be strong, take the chance.
Do the moves, proudly prance.

You have grace, you have poise.
Just forget about the noise.

Do the kip, do the flip,
Do the backbend on the floor
Perform a handspring and a round off
'Cause the audience wants more.

In gymnastics, you've got to want it.
Once you learn a trick, you flaunt it.
But everybody messes up,
They miss a beat, or trip.
But don't give up and don't give in
'Cause everybody slips.

And now the judges tally scores and then…
You bite your lip and twirl your hair…
They've given you a… ten!

Holly Miller
*Lexington, SC*

## Autumn Colors

Blazing red the maples, orange are the ash,
yellow leaves on birches, join the autumn bash.
Defiant are the evergreens, standing green and tall,
refusing to celebrate, the coming of the fall.

Autumn colors fall from branches, to the canvas on the ground.
Painting autumn landscapes, the portraits are profound.
Quilted color patches blanket hillsides rising high,
flaunting awesome colors, at the deep blue autumn sky.

Shafts of brilliant sunlight and bursting colors play.
The autumn holds us captive and takes our breath away.
They rustle in the wind, then fade and start to fly,
autumn colors letting go, and bidding us good-bye.

John Hutchinson
*Whitingham, VT*

## Grandma Lillian

I miss her laugh…
I miss her smile…
I miss her dearly…
Remembering her always
I can still see her
She loves us dearly
And we love her
We always blow kisses at the sky
When we pass by, we imagine her
We all can't go through a day without her in our minds
Tears come down our cheeks for,
She has left this earth
But,
Will never leave our hearts

Kaylee Briggs
*Roseville, CA*

# Listen with Your Heart

Every moment of every day,
We can make a difference.
We make life a beautiful art,
When we listen with our heart.

See that person down the street,
Who's angry with his neighbor?
He's quick to judge,
And thinks he's right,
Won't take time to listen.
Instead, he'd rather arm for fight.
Compromise, beyond his vision.

See the children in the park.
They learned well from their parents,
"Don't let people bother you,
With what is wrong or right.
If with you, they don't agree,
Stand your ground and fight."
Compromise, beyond their vision.

The message to be learned from this,
Is never be judgmental.
Take the time to listen well,
For we don't walk this earth alone,
Of troubles we all can tell.
So understand and compromise,
To end this world's division.

Nancy Lauzon
*Salem, WI*

*I am a retired elementary school teacher and the author of two children's books. I have been writing poetry since I was in high school. I have been frustrated with how people are so quick to form opinions and judge others without knowing anything about them. People do not listen to each other, so they do not realize what challenges others may have. This poem is my way of touching others, helping them to understand how they can make a positive difference in the world, one person at a time.*

## Secret

I have a secret
burning deep within.
It claws
It screams
But I can never let it go
This secret deep within
I'll never let anyone know.

Elizabeth Rebecca Leber
*Lake Charles, LA*

## The War

The wind howls through the woods as the lone wolf should.
The hubbub of the city is replaced by the words of a witty
  spokesman.
The hum of machinery dissolves into the thrum of artillery and war.
The dreams of a child are shattered through the means of vile nature.
The peace of a nation is destroyed through the beast of temptation.
The hope of a people turns to dust in the face of a ravaged steeple.
And yet life strives on.
The love in a beating heart is replenished by another's doting part.
The joy that tears at man's deepest despairs and a human's will to
  continue to fill the vast, empty voids of fear with cheer, are all
  reasons life strives on.

Blakely Naylor
*Murray, UT*

## Bethlehem Baby

Marble structures seem divine.
Painted pictures, hearts entwine.
People gaze at monuments,
Rock, concrete, and steel.
A torch burns in the wilderness
For governments to steal.
Flesh torn into ivory, fingers bleed the prayer
A baby born in Bethlehem, nobody seems to care.
Harp strings fly the words of peace.
Incense burns below.
The choir sings the hope of love,
As the world turns so cold.
A silver box in the cardinal's hand,
Reflected in a book.
A voice in the microphone praises the babe.
Baptism in the brook.
Government and religion
When they act as one,
Results in war, and the score
Is always none to none.

It's clear to me why people feel
Apathy, and they despair.
A baby born in Bethlehem,
Nobody seems to care.

Mark Franko
*Hutchinson, KS*

# Spring

Bright, sunny, breezy,
Blooming, budding, sneezy.
Stormy, dark clouds, rainbows.
Gardening, tilling, fixing rows,
Planting seeds, watch them grow.
Children playing, flying kites,
Running, jumping, riding bikes.
Mowing grass, setting out trees,
Fixing flower beds down on our knees.
Longer days, shorter nights
O — springtime, what a delight!

Lorraine Curley
*Eure, NC*

## Memories

I spent my early childhood, in mid Tennessee,
I guess that is the reason, those hills are dear to me.
I go back for a visit every chance I get,
I have beautiful memories there that I won't forget.
I met my first girlfriend there, her name was Mary Ann,
We rode the school bus and, I held her hand.
Then I moved away, and we never got to see,
How our lives evolved, or what we came to be.

Pascol Abner
*Sylacauga, AL*

## 29 and Holdin'

Ready, set, go —

Birth to 29
Seem to be the best years
Beyond too many fears
So I'm 29 and holdin'
Though the future be unfoldin'

Looking back brings memories
And fears flee from me
I'm a kid without a care,
Still had my hair, even went to the fair,
Was able to climb the stairs
So I'm 29 and holdin'

Oh the starry nights and the kisses good-night
Everything seemed right

29 and holdin' that's where I'll be
If chance you're lookin' for me

If Heaven has numerous gates
And over each door number plates
Number 29 will be mine
Member to tell 'em
I'm 29 and holdin'

Beverly Burrow
*Clarendon, TX*

*Advancing in age myself made me think of what my father-in-law replied when asked how old he was; it was, "I'm twenty-nine!" As years passed, he was always twenty-nine. So here I am twice twenty-nine already and I thought, I'm not the only one. So you guessed it, I'm twenty-nine and holdin'. As life deals weary news, I figured a little chuckle might make life lighter.*

# Then and Now

New modern trends don't much appeal to me,
I prefer to reminisce about the way things used to be.
If you're wistfully dreamin' of being born a hundred years too late,
You can't fix it pardner, 'cause you're plumb outta date.

But still, I like to roam through museums,
And contemplate the items restored and displayed;
The tools and implements, of some past trade,
Now vastly improved from the old handmade.

There are many organizations, that will endeavor,
To keep some old time ways and traditions forever.
Researching the past to learn the "when and how,"
Providing separate cases for the "then and now."

In this way they can, for others, entertain.
But there are some things you don't need to explain.
In Hebrews 13:8, it says, that Jesus Christ is
"The same yesterday, today and forever."

This helps me to keep a proper perspective,
Regarding "when and how" and "then and now."
And yet I still enjoy reminiscing again,

"Every now and then!"

Clifford Shinn
*Nampa, ID*

## Person in the Mirror

Something strange or even queer
About the person in the mirror

Stranger yet in every way
There's a different person every day

Once if standing on tiptoes
All that was seen was forehead and nose

A few years later someone taller has taken his place
About to put a razor to his face

Suddenly there's a face that almost beams
Handsome — like we picture in our dreams

Then almost like magic without warning
Someone disheveled and unkempt in the morning

However with slight of hand and some TLC
We see the face we want it to be

Then over a shoulder a beautiful face appears
One that's been there through the years

Now a few others on tiptoes
Hoping to see more than forehead and nose

Now the person in the mirror is almost bald I fear
With more and more wrinkles appearing each year

A single person in the mirror once more
With two days' stubble and wrinkles galore

Now the person is haggard and bent
Thinking each day alive is heaven-sent

Now there's no longer a person in the mirror
It hangs alone longingly awaiting another to appear

Edward F. Shaffer
*Hagerstown, MD*

# Irish Ardor

Canopy covers—
verdant lands.
Sheer cliffs drop
where castles stand.

Fortifying soils
that stem,
colorful sprouts—
masterful gems.

Path indirect,
heart recaptured.
Lost time found,
a soul enraptured.

Susan Williams
*Orlando, FL*

*Susan Williams is a freelance writer living in Orlando, Florida, with her husband and two boys. "Irish Ardor" is inspired by Ireland, a magical country, and embedded in the poem's lines is a love unrealized. She believes with every published poem, a seed of human awareness is planted.*

## A Shade for Life

In our small backyard stands a cherimoya tree
With its spreading branches as a shade for me
There I recall the memories of my childhood
With some good friends and a cozy neighborhood

When I am lonesome for being alone
No one to talk to or to tag along
Sitting under its branches gives me an inspiration
To have a better, longer life in spite of being alone

Fe A. Vilches
*Torrance, CA*

## My Haiku

*Grey's Anatomy*
Lying, live, love, life, lost
Dreaming, breathing, gone

Alaina Carlone
*Canton, OH*

*I am thirteen and am in eighth grade at St. Michael's School in Canton, OH. I am the youngest of three siblings, Marisa being the oldest and Brianna in the middle. I have a dog named Oreo, a Shetland sheep dog. I love* Grey's Anatomy *and* Grimm. *Cristina Yang was my favorite character from* Grey's Anatomy. *My teacher, Mrs. Stuhlmiller, introduced me to this contest and I am really glad she did. I am going to be published and I hope it will happen again. I just wanted to say thanks to everybody, whether I mentioned you or not. Thank you!*

## Holiday Memories

Christmas Eve, the holidays are here
Starring Santa, and his famous reindeer
Down the chimney, quietly he will creep
Bearing gifts, while everyone is sound asleep
Early Christmas morning, scurrying to see
Beautifully wrapped gifts, under the tree
Excited to open, each a surprising delight
Thanks to Santa, for sleighing, the cold winter night
Warmed by the fire, the logs all aglow
Singing Christmas carols, then frolicking in the snow
Etching wings of angels, or sledding down a hill
Wishing this joyful day, could magically stand still
But the day skips by, as the night draws near
Holding these memories, till more are made next year

Elizabeth Steinhoff
*Huntley, IL*

# A Walk of Faith

*Through many trials and errors*
*I walk several miles of prayers*
As I exalt Christ upon high
A flowing river of joyful tears I will cry
For even in the darkest place
His mighty light still shines a loving grace
One so powerful no one can compare
I will commend His name, and never despair
Sometimes life can bring a raging fire
An abundance of faith it might require
I magnify my credence, and it will soon expire
As I courageously walk in life with a God fearing heart
My intense loyalty shows of hope
A new beginning which anyone can start
Be not afraid, humble yourselves and grab the rope
Oh what I have learned from the thunder's deep roar
In a time of need I knock, and opened will be the door
And boldly from the mouth a glorifying praise will pour
With the wise understanding of heavenly peace
The Holy Spirit in our lives can wildly increase
By believing in Christ I will fiercely declare
And knowing the importance of just one prayer
In my life He is always on the highest throne
I stand bravely knowing I am never alone
*Through many trials and errors*
*I walk several miles of prayers*

JaNae M. Dennis
*Casper, WY*

*My name is JaNae Dennis. I am from Casper, Wyoming. I have been writing songs and poetry since I was very young. The Lord has blessed me with a genuine way of writing and a strong family that is very loyal and supportive. God's love and grace is what inspired me to write "A Walk of Faith." The Lord did not promise that life would be easy, but He did promise us His Holy Spirit, who is our comfort, hope, joy, peace, and understanding, etc. We have been given the grace to believe. That is why we walk by faith.*

## Auto Crazy

Wonder why unemployment climbs high?
Just look at the supermarket where you buy.
An automatic checkout has replaced,
Where once there was a smiling face.
At the bank machines are counting money,
When they break, the scene is far from funny.
Sadly, a teller is almost obsolete too,
An ATM greets you as you drive through.
At the airport you must check yourself in,
Finding human assistance is pretty slim.
Choose your own seat and pay through the nose,
This is progress? How modern life goes.
Choose a hotel room online,
Don't know computers: you're in a bind.
A telemarketing machine calls your phone line,
Hawking products of every color and kind.
Creating jobs for Americans no more,
Many companies are fleeing offshore.
Free trade's goal was to sell our things,
Not the greedy enjoying the money it brings,
At the expense of the American worker bee,
Required to toil longer for less in the land of the free.

Illene G. Powell
*Myrtle Beach, SC*

## Merry Baby Christmas

Babies, *babies*, everywhere!
Crawling here, *crawling* there!
Look over here... look over there...
One's under the table; one's standing in a chair!
   And as for me, I just stand and stare!

The toys are scattered all over the floor...
The house is just a big *eyesore*!
(There comes another kid in the door!)
Surely they cannot bring any more...
   There are five more now than the year before.

Stop! Don't eat the berries off the wreath!
Go take a nap... we need some relief.
We don't even have time to breathe.
(I wonder what time they all will leave...
   Maybe it will be soon... I won't grieve.)

One has pulled over the tree...
Where did he go? I cannot see!
Did he belong to you, or belong to me?
Let's go count... oops... there are only three.
   Maybe Santa can find him under that tree.

But all in all, we'll have *good cheer*...
The long-lost relatives will soon be here.
And they'll eat all the food. *Never fear!*
How wonderful to look forward to another year!
   Merry Christmas, *one and all.*

Yvonne E. Cole
*Villa Rica, GA*

*Yvonne Eaves Cole and her husband, Charles Cole, have three children, five grandchildren, and five great-grandchildren. She is a native of Georgia. Christmas is so much fun when the babies are "everywhere" and into "everything," so her poem is a natural response to holiday family gatherings.*

# I Didn't Know

I didn't know that it *would* feel this way.
I didn't know that it *could* feel this way.
I didn't know what it would really
Feel like without you.
I'm sad, and my heart is lonely.
I'm sad, and my heart feels blue.
I'm so sad, I'm already missing you.
The tears I cry are tears of sorrow.
The tears I shed are tears of pain.
I look around, and you're not here with me.
I didn't know.
I didn't know that it would be so lonely.
I didn't know that I could feel so homeless.
I didn't know how it would really be.
I sigh and breathe a little deeper.
I sigh and look all around me.
Nothing is the same since you aren't here with me.
I didn't know.
It's been so long since I felt lonely.
It's been so long since I was all alone.
And now I know that I need to belong to you.
I dry my eyes and take a deep breath.
I dry my eyes; my soul begins to rest.
I feel a peace that comforts me inside.
I know that I am much alive, and I know that I,
I will survive.

Alicia G. Smith-Mackall
*Jacksonville, NC*

*"I Didn't Know" is one of seventy-eight poems published in my first book,* From My Heart to Your Heart, *in March 2013. This poem was birthed during a heartfelt moment after my husband Robert and I moved to North Carolina. He accepted a job and had to go away for training, leaving me home alone, for the first time in our eight years of marriage, for six months. The thoughts of him not coming back were quite traumatic. I know many military families and those who have lost a loved one can relate to this feeling of loneliness and sadness.*

## Breathe

This place
This place some think is poor and so devoid of grace,
Sits high and cupped, like Shangri-La
Within the mountain's green embrace.

Be still.
Hear.
Lapping waves of an ancient ghostly sea.
There… shimmering, just out of sight
Where now grow sage and tumbleweed.

And I
Who felt as old as rock
Moved from somewhere else.
To here.
To breathe.

S. Pritchard
*White Sulphur Springs, MT*

*Against all good advice, I retired and this California native moved to a place as foreign as the moon. I didn't think I could live so far from the ocean but when I look down into our little valley and feel the wind running off the sage, the sea is there. This may well not be the last place I live, but for now it will do.*

## Halloween

The night is dark as pitch black coal
The air is still and fills my soul
With memories of bygone days
Of chanting ghost and haunted graves
The clanging of the chains that bind
The sounds that overwhelmed my mind
The flying witch, the shrieking cat
The headless horseman, the vampire bat
The pumpkin with his smile so keen
Reminders all of Halloween

Mary Alice Causey
*Casselberry, FL*

## The Gift

I hear the tap, tap on the window as it tries to gain entry.
I see the flowers smiling as they close their petals for the day.
The air smells fresh and the grass is greener.
My water bill will be smaller.
My nap is sounder and all is well with the world.
What a great gift God has given us today: rain!

Veronica Suchan
*Yorba Linda, CA*

*I was seventy-nine when I joined a free writing class at the senior center. It was on Tuesday afternoon for eight weeks. I wrote poems, short stories, and family history for my children and grandchildren. It seldom rains in Southern California so when I heard the tap, tap on my window I wrote the poem.*

## Winter Memories

I remember when I was young
catching snowflakes on my tongue
    floating
    swirling
    dancing

I remember the terrific thrill
of feeling that cold winter chill
    knit cap
    warm gloves
    wool coat

I remember having a fun snow fight
watching all the snowballs take flight
    throwing
    shouting
    laughing

I remember the snowman we built
corncob pipe and a hat at a tilt
    button eyes
    carrot nose
    red scarf

I remember making angels in the snow
it really doesn't seem so long ago
    falling back
    arms moving
    legs swinging

wonderful childhood memories

Sharon L. Howard
*San Jose, CA*

## Stay on Line

God's line never busy—talk to Him today,
If you feel troubled or in dismay.
He's always there with a listening ear,
Be patient—answers you're sure to hear.

If problems tend not to cease,
Stay on line and ask Him for peace.
He will ask you not to get bitter,
Stay on line and things will get better.

Strengthen your day—pray out loud,
Look to Heaven through peaceful clouds.
Your personal triumphs sure to be won,
Things will be better when this you have done.

So always keep Him in your mind,
Pray and leave your troubles behind.
Stay on line and pray from your heart,
In His name—less troubles will start.

Give thanks for His guidance and strength,
Be it short or long in its length.
Pick up the phone and give Him a call,
His line always open—for one—for all.

Marlene Neubauer
*Glidden, IA*

*I was born in Carroll, Iowa, in 1937. I grew up on a small farm near Glidden, Iowa. I attended a one-room country school, graduating after eight years, and then went on to high school. Jack and I have been married fifty-nine years. We have been very blessed with five daughters, two sons and nineteen grand and great-grandchildren. It has been my dream to have some of my poems published. I enjoy expressing my thoughts in verse. This poem I've written warms my heart and I hope it will warm your heart also.*

## Wooded Country Paths

Walking carefree down a country lane observing everything along
the way
Watching the small animals scurrying here and there under the
leaves and over the grassy paths
Collecting seeds and nuts to hide and store for the long cold winter
that is just ahead
Listening to the buzz of the busy bees darting into the wild flowers
collecting nectar to store in their hives
Watching and listening on the country paths realizing everything is
so alive
The chirping and singing of the many colorful birds fluttering and
flying to and fro
The songs they sing is music to our ears
When they sense us they will scatter hiding in the trees showing a
little fear
We are intruders for just a while longer and all the creatures are
watching us as if they know that we are the ones who don't
belong here on their wooded country paths

Rosalie Kurtz
*Columbiana, OH*

# Lies

Lies start out innocent and clean
But in time lies grow big and mean

Lies get tangled like a web
Making it easy to tell another fib

One lie builds on another
And it keeps going in even further

The lies pile up
And it is hard to tell which end is up

Sometimes lies are told to keep from supposedly hurting someone
But in reality the lying hurts everyone

The lies eventually get uncovered
And when confronted more lies are told to be protected

How can someone look you in the eye
And continue daily to lie

A liar will sadly never change
So go ahead and accept the pain

In the end lying does not pay
Now we must go our separate ways

Cheryl Bono
*Onley, VA*

*Cheryl Bono lives on the Eastern Shore of Virginia where she has worked in the education field for twenty-three years. Currently she serves as a high school counselor. Cheryl previously worked as an elementary teacher and a middle school counselor. She graduated from Salisbury State University in 1991 with a degree in elementary education. In 1998, she received a master's degree in school counseling from the University of Maryland Eastern Shore. Cheryl writes poetry as a purpose to express her emotions creatively. She encourages everyone to use self expression through some form of writing. She plans to pursue her doctorate.*

# The Unsettled Soul

Where to go, what to do
Never know until hindsight catches up to you, hindsight catches up
For that's the tale of the unsettled soul, an unsettled soul is he

He that has fallen short from all that he has dreamt
He that feels he was meant for more
When his tears are the cause of a flood
All because his dreams flooded with more, more dreams than before

He that hasn't reached his destination in which he was destined
He that feels a sliver of emptiness, in the void of his heart
When his yells are the cause of the storm
All because he thought his destination would fill that sliver, that
sliver with more

He that cannot find that in which he is in search of
He that feels he should have loved more
When his thoughts are the cause of darkness
All because his love leads him to darkness, to darkness more

Where to go, what to do
Never know until hindsight catches up to you, hindsight catches up
For that's the tale of the unsettled soul, an unsettled soul is he

Jill Ramirez
*Iron River, MI*

# Gradoo

Gradoo, what's that!
Is that something Dr. Seuss
would say to Cat?
No, it's crud, dirt, gunk or whatever
you might have.
What should I do with the gradoo?
Make sure it's not on my shoe!

Janice Preece
*Glens Falls, NY*

# Untitled

Ignore the drama.
Make new friends.
Avoid the haters.
Start new trends.
And never make the same mistakes over and over again.

Haley Farris
*Kinston, AL*

*I am fourteen and my parents are Brad and LyDonna Farris. My sister, Paige Farris, is seventeen. I wrote this poem to encourage people to be who they are, regardless of what people say and think. Stand out if you want to. Don't follow trends, start them. Be yourself. Be you. Do what makes you happy, not what makes everyone else happy. People are always going to hate and make fun. You just have to ignore it. Love who you are. Never stop making new friends. Just don't make the mistake of giving second chances to people who don't deserve them.*

## In the Glimmering Eyes of a Child

In the glimmering eyes of a child
Hope is seen as a possibility,
Where dreams are embraced as friends,
And goals never clouded by reality.

Within the pure spirit of a child
Is a heart that beats with anticipation,
Like the clean flowing spring of a fountain,
Life flows through, sending nourishment to the soul.

Within the loving arms of a child,
Eternity is embraced by a tender grasp,
The heavens look down and smile,
And all of creation is blessed and renewed.

Deborah LaPier
*Omaha, NE*

## Life

Layer upon layer
Swirl by swirl
Patterning the memories
Time
Laughter within tears
Joy upon pain
Sculpturing into love
Time
Raindrops instead of diamonds
Struggle versus ease
Painting my tapestry
Time
Life ignores death
Faith welcomes resurrection
Creating our miracles
Time

Madge Reilly
*Staten Island, NY*

## Birthday Balloon

Youthful celebrant's ephemeral delight,
Rainbow-hued sphere, puffed as a perigee moon,
Iridescent pinks and shimmering silver,
Festive greeting ornately etched in graceful script.
Icarus-like, vainly attempting to scale the heavens,
With sporadic tugs at its glittering, tightly held cord,
Helium-intoxicated bounces of thwarted escapes.
Gravity-defying party favor, flashing glints of light.

*Twenty-four hours later*

Abandoned in the gutter, earth-bound and forgotten,
Deflating like the melting remains of an ice cream cake.
Brilliant colors paled by filthy rainwater,
Grit-smeared letters blurred as memories of sparkling yesterdays,
Once gleaming tether torn and opaque with mud,
About to be crushed by the wheel of a speeding car,
Driven by an indifferent and uncaring motorist.
Birthday balloon
To the jaded and insensitive, disposable luminescence.

Bette Cyzner
*Forest Hills, NY*

# Invisible Woman

The other day when I was out,
I noticed people were moving about.
Not one looked my way, not even to say,
Good morning and have a nice day.

Those that looked in my direction,
looked through me with no affection.
I sat down on a bench to ponder and see,
And wonder just what has happened to me.

I remember when I was young and pretty,
I could turn heads in the country or the city.
The looks weren't limited from just the male gender,
Even females checked me out and they were tender.

Now as I see my full reflection,
My skin is spotted and my eyes no reaction.
The hair is thin, dull and full of grey,
And my energy is stuck on low every day.

It dawned on me when you reached the sixties,
Women become invisible, and that's not nifty.
If those folks only knew what I know to share,
I could make people's lives fun with care.

But look a little closer you could see,
The forever young person hiding in me.
Books, music and life lessons I could share to all,
All of us would have an absolute life-altering ball,

If you would look at invisible women at all.

Grace Frasche'
*Citrus Heights, CA*

*I was eight years old living in Virginia when I discovered the world of poetry in the school library. My favorite author was Ogden Nash. I have always been intrigued with rhyming words and have written poetry off and on for years based on what was going on in my life at the time. I've gone through a lot of life lessons with the help of family and friends. I have discovered that life is a book that is rewritten everyday and doesn't have a final chapter. I currently reside in California.*

# The Journey

There she is again, clouding up my mind,
I wish I could untangle the ties that bind.
The web that weaves my child to me,
Has become unglued from the lure of a fantasy.
The hollowness that fills her once radiant eyes,
Tells me that the binding tie is slipping by.
To fill that craving that distracts her healthy thoughts,
She must delve into the world of battles which cannot be fought.
The fuzziness and the fake peace of mind is only short lived,
Then the craving hole is empty and she must find a way to refill.
I am on my knees, with my hands lifted high,
Hoping for a quick answer from the master in the sky.
What can I do, what can I say
That will take her away from those who pull her farther away?
The highs of available demonical supplies and the lows of
being without,
Have taken a toll on the one who was brave and stout.
All choices have consequences, one must learn for sure,
But they get tangled up in that side of life which is impure.
So the black robed one slams the gavel on the wood,
And my child walks away with a look of "I wish I had understood."
The curtain has fallen, she sleeps in a place of strange sounds,
I hope she can hear me quietly singing, as I try to quiet the heart
that pounds.
I can feel the web weaving her back to me, the doors will open and
set her free.
She will be running and so will I, laughing and crying at the
same time.
The journey has ended, forever I hope,
She remains my child, and I will find a way to cope.

Linda Wells
*Hixson, TN*

## Grief Versus Time

Grief doesn't go away because
loss doesn't go away
Time permits me to grieve
less intensely — less often
Time permits me to move from
memories to the future
It is a journey everyone will travel
The route taken is individual…
The timing indefinite, but
a brighter future is possible —
given time

Rita Rose Marcinek
*Johnstown, PA*

*People's seemingly judgmental views and indifferent attitudes about dealing with major loss inspired my poem, "Grief Versus Time." It is a myth that "time" alone will take away one's grief. It's what we do with the time that counts. My husband died unexpectedly two and a half years ago. He was three weeks from retiring from a teaching career. A family member became a victim of a homicide twenty-two years ago. Since those dark days in my life, I've become an advocate for victims of crime and those grieving a personal loss. I hope my poem will dispel the myth of time taking away grief.*

## I Wonder How

Have you ever wondered how,
  Milk is made inside the cow?
During sleep, cows must dream
  About making milk and cream.
And grass and water eaten by cows,
  Magically, becomes milk somehow.
And according to my mother,
  Milk gets stored in their udders.

Did you know some farmers allow
  People to watch them milking cows?
And when cows hear music or songs
  They give more milk and moo along.
Cows are able to walk through mud,
  And spend hours chewing their cud.
But every cow's claim to fame
  Is that she has her own name.

Have you ever wondered how,
  Life might be without the cow?
  No milk for your oatmeal
  Or cream cheese on bagels.
  No pizza or toasted cheese
  Or butter on bread or peas.
  No pudding or yogurt
  Or ice cream for dessert.
So, perhaps, all people should vow
  To thank the farmer and the cow.

Helen Keck
*Winston Salem, NC*

## Jihadist

The locust are coming.
The locust are swarming.
Jihadists are locust!
Their king is Abbadon.
They are demon possessed.
They all feed on hatred.
They eat hate for breakfast,
for lunch
and
for dinner.
And all the time between
they're coming after *you*!
And
they're coming after *me*!
So
be
very
very
*green.*

Eleanor Harkey
*Grass Valley, CA*

*I am widowed with four independent children. I'm one hundred percent Irish, a retired first-grade teacher, and will be eighty on May 31, 2015. When I read Rev. 9:1–12, I knew it meant "Jihadist" which means fighting holy wars and doing God's will, ISIS, etc. "Men" believe this; therefore, I should have added after the third line, "Holy war, holy fake!" God has given me a wonderful, intimate knowledge of his word. Some will say, "That's not very humble. Who do you think you are, the Queen of Sheba?" Matt 12:42 and Luke 11:31. I say, "Time will tell—won't it?"*

## Soar

warm… content…
her river flows —
currents cleanse, pure spirit whole

Dreams like
rapids roar — high
above,
beyond reach
soar

Oh, how her soul did smile,
how her heart glowed with warmth —
when once his face appeared…
no strength to hold back desires to be
forever entwined… he and she
(though memories trace the land,
free again the shore will end)

Erin Antonino
*Methuen, MA*

# Miro

When I walk through the dining room
Or wake up in my bed
I think of all the things you did,
And all the things you said.

So now I must move forward,
And hold my head up high.
But now I miss you oh so much,
And always want to cry.

I held you when you looked at me.
I held you when you shook.
I loved you oh so very much
My heart you always took.

Our time was really way too short
And now I miss you badly.
If I could do it all again,
I would do it very gladly.

I loved you oh so very much.
You were my little boy.
When you came into my life,
You filled my life with joy.

Now all you are is in my heart.
Your memory oh so bright.
You must know now that I'm okay.
I'll see you in the light.

Garnett Brooks
*Port Townsend, WA*

*My cat, Miro, was late in years. He was somewhat set in his ways. He was faced with traveling in the cab of a truck to Chicago. Then he was dumped on me. He, right from the beginning, clung to me. I became the "stable" in his ever changing world. I was early in my recovery from a twenty-three-year meth addiction. He accepted me unconditionally. I loved him. One day, I woke up with Miro on my right side. He was staring at me when I opened my eyes. I knew then that we were in love.*

## Heads Down

We live in a society of heads down
  Not in prayer
  Not in contemplation
  Not in remorse
We connect or disconnect electronically
  Not face to face
  Not eye to eye
  Not heart to heart
Look around
  Heads down in restaurants
  Heads down in stores
  Heads down while driving
And sadly
  Heads down at home

A society filled with heads down
  cannot see where it's going
The solution is simple, but perhaps
  already unattainable

Heads up

Charlotte Brown
*Oak Forest, IL*

## To My Mother

Heaven knows that I love my mother;
She's the one that gave me birth,
The one God chose in His great plan
To give me life on earth.
She believed in God and shared His love;
She was always giving or helping everyone:
She taught her children about God through church and her faith.
She was always there for us and made sure we were safe.
Mother worked hard to give us a good life
To make sure we had what we need
After all she had nine children to feed.
Mother always did more than her share
Everyone she met or was near she showed them she cared.
My father left us and gave no support,
But Mother still kept all nine of us together with the love in her heart,
And as we grew older and had our own children
She kept us together with "family gatherings" and "holiday meals."
My mother is gone now to Heaven,
She died of dementia and Alzheimer's disease.
I love her so much and even though there were days she did not
remember me
I miss and remember all of the times we were together.
In my heart she is still with me yard-saling, enjoying hot
fudge sundae,
Or we are just going for a walk.
I know she is waiting for me, and that is just one more reason
I want to be all she taught me to be and share the love gave
so generously.

Marietta Hearn
*St. Louis, MO*

# Ode to Linda

The "Dam-if-I-no" was traveling real slow,
Next to the big Penrod rig,
When all of a sudden without any warning,
There came a marlin so big.

A lure it did take—it wanted no bait,
As Linda grabbed onto the rod.
For two hours and a half, it avoided the gaff,
Then came up with nary a nod.

The men of the Gulf were all quite appalled,
That a lady could land such a fish.
For years they had tried—some even had died,
Trying to fulfill such a wish.

To Port Eads they did go with the marlin in tow,
A thousand-eighteen read the scale.
The people all cheered as they weighed in the fish
A new tournament queen they did hail.

Judith W. Greene
*Brandon, FL*

*In the summer of 1977, a woman named Linda Koener was fishing in the New Orleans Big Game Fishing Club Woman's Tournament. She caught a 1,018 pound blue marlin, the largest marlin ever caught on rod and reel in the Gulf of Mexico by a man or woman. I was also fishing in the tournament with my husband, Roger, and Isabel and Tommy Faust. When we heard about Linda's big catch, I was so excited, I wrote this poem for her. I read "Ode to Linda" to her that night at the award's banquet.*

# What Made Me

I wouldn't say my home has made me who I am.
I wouldn't say this school has made me who I am.
I wouldn't say this city has made me who I am.
These are just places, buildings, areas, and pieces of land.
This state doesn't care about us, he or she,
And this country doesn't even know about me.
North America is just a large piece of nature,
But this is not me or my true creator.
The planet that we all call Earth,
Even if it was the place of my birth,
It doesn't have feelings or a nurturing heart,
But splits up our cultures so far apart.
All these places have not made me,
No, for it is the people,
They have made me who I want to be.
From the ones that live inside my home,
And comfort me when I feel alone.
To the students and faculty in school,
They know that I will be no one's fool
This diverse population in this city and state,
Helps me to decide my life and fate.
Every single person in the USA
Has shown some support in their own way.
So take a look at everything and you might just see,
It's a small piece of all—that has created me…

Derek Routhier
*Brockton, MA*

# The Pursuit of Infinity

I've come to a realization at the ripe age of twenty-two, the pre-twilight of my existence. The realization was simple, seemingly staring me in the face. We people are creatures of excess. Moderation is our flaw and subtlety is our most scarce trait. Never thinking of tomorrow but only living in the now. Our ego driven line in the sand, only to get washed away by the very time we fight to outrun. I stand humbled in the shadows of the passing sun. Who am I but a fleeting voice, and that's the real discovery. We can try to hold more than our arms may bear but we will never cease to fight for more. We are specks of dust shining in the light of dead stars light-years away. We love underdogs, we cheer for impossibility. The human race is exactly that, a race: an eternal competition to best others only because we fear failure. Victory is never enough, fortune is never enough, and happiness is never enough. I've looked at my dog as a simple creature of basic needs. For whom scraps of food can convert an ordinary day into a moment of pure bliss. Spontaneity and optimism in their truest forms. It must be nice.

Kevin Archila-Vargas
*Parsippany, NJ*

# Spoiled

Fall asleep on my mother's lap
and my pencil-thin, long legs hit the floor.
Special breakfast of pancakes and chocolate milk.
For dinner, spinach from a can, a fried chicken wing,
and a slice of Wonder Bread with the crust cut off.
Served first. My yellow plate with tiny red ladybugs
along the edges sits next to my favorite drink,
grape Kool-Aid in a jelly jar.

When mother's friends with children visit,
we entertain them. I share my paper dolls, tea set
and coloring books. For a short while, I am mother's
perfect co-hostess. Then, I get restless and want the
children to go home. I want my regular routine.
Play grown-up and prance around in my oldest sister's patent leather
high heels. Drape mother's old pink flowered house-dress
around my twiggy body and pretend it's an evening gown.
Check a dusty brown handbag for sticks of Juicy Fruit gum.

Most of the time, mother belongs to me, but lately I have to
share her. Four older brothers, four shotgun weddings,
and four wives abandon my nieces and nephews.
My brothers and their children move home with us.
Too many people, too many changes make me
a sissy bully, a selfish giver, and a spoiled fresh-mouth.
But at bedtime, I fall asleep on our mother's lap
and my pencil-thin, long legs hit the floor.

Aressa V. Williams
*Upper Marlboro, MD*

## Uniquely Yours

When you make way for love, everyday
of the week, when you start each day
with love, world brimming with love.
  When you step out in love dewdrops
of sweetness, when you embrace the world
with your love, the finest, uniquely yours,
atmosphere of sweetness, your love in the
brilliant of light, breathtaking beautiful
pleasant and sweet, striking beautiful,
lovely, delightful.  The perfect place is
in your heart, filled with love, sunny disposition.
There are many splendors, you bring the inside
out, sunny world filled with love.
One of the surest ways to create the moods,
is with the light of love, dazzling light
of love, just and right, beautiful and bright,
grand.  Solid love, sweet tranquility,
vast array of beauty.  Unlimited loving, lot of
love, path of sweetness, your brilliant
light of love.  When it comes to love
you got it yes, uniquely yours.

Mae Nell James
*Dearborn, MI*

## Heaven Is Really There

But by invitation only
Cannot buy a ticket

God is the gate keeper
Your soul is payment

Living by God's will
And doing His work is required

If He chooses you
You will surely go into the light

Everlasting love will abound you
Forever and forever

Christine M. Brice
*West Lawn, PA*

## Nations of Love

Why can't we all be
Friendly nations?
We need to shake hands
With brotherly
Love!
Gardens should grow
In our wonderful
Land!
Not bloodshed and
Desolation to name
A few!
When we all join in
Prayer to our wonderful
Savior,
God will heal our land
And bless every
Nation.
Peace will take hold
And all will be
Well.

Patricia Jelsomine
*Westmont, IL*

# The Name of the Game

What do you do when you're old, and almost gray?
Living alone, even the cat went away
Life looking drabber than any-thing-o
Why, you discover, a thing called BINGO!

Now I'm busy most every night
Marking cards with dabbers bright
Making friends, and new cohorts
While practicing our "favorite sport"

My good luck charms, sitting in a row
Money on the table—that's a no-no
A new language, I now spout
"I'm cased," "I'm set," and the ever popular, "sock it out"

I try not to be overzealous
I try not to be over-jealous
But now that I've learned the rules and the lingo
When do I get to holler—*BINGO!*

Mary K. Moore
*Stillwater, NY*

## My Mother

A woman at forty-five
Still very much alive
Run, run, work all day…
For her it is the only way
Jitterbug, tango at the dance
Britson legs on the prance
Extravagant in her fur of mink
Smiling rosy cheeks of pink
My mother, like no other,
Lives today for another

Paul DiLallo
*Redondo Beach, CA*

## A Tribute to My Daughter Gina Marie

A stem to my rose Gina is to me
So loving and caring — no one else could ever be
Direct, honest and strong —
In my eyes she absolutely does no wrong
A woman of status — no doubt
Working very hard and running about
So many things about her I so adore
So Gina my precious daughter
Stay with me I implore!

Mary Ann Caruso
*Laurel, MD*

# Crimson Victory

The golden red ruby sinks in the West and beckons forms of
Nature to rest.
A waning moon lists high on its beam inviting to slumber—the
hills and streams.
Twilight gazes at the earth just dim as star dust gathers on the
Dipper's rim
And up in the towers the chimes ring clear as the call of the lark
homing its dear.
But far away—in some land unknown no lark commands his
quiet home.
No towers tall—with shades of rose no mountain stream can
find repose.
The harmony of shells begins and fades away on traveled winds
The cries of the wounded fallen in droves—hallow his soul who
never arose.
Waves creep silently on the sand and fade the crimson of its strands.
And the graves that are dug and filled again are never touched by
human whim.
Now twilight falls with Nature's hood and comes to rest where
brave men
stood. And the golden ruby begins to gleam but now must pass
away unseen.

John Maluso Sr.
*Canfield, OH*

*John Maluso Sr. is ninety years young, and is a retired educator from Youngstown, OH. He was a teacher, speech and hearing therapist, principal of two high schools, coordinator of speech education, and director of pupil personnel services. He retired in 1985 at the age of sixty-two and became a member of the Youngstown Board of Education for eight years, the last four as president. John Maluso has been an avid writer of poetry and short stories since he was a young man. His submission here, "Crimson Victory," was written during his time as a Seabee in the Navy, in WWII while serving in Guadalcanal. He remains active in his community, along with his wife of sixty-four years, Claire Maluso. They have two married children and two grandchildren. John continues to write and has volumes of poems and short stories he has shared with family and friends for many years.*

# For Those Soldiers

This is for those soldiers
who left home to fight.
This is for those soldiers
who are doing what's right.
This is for those soldiers
who sacrifice their life.
This is for those soldiers
who give their all tonight.
This is for those soldiers
who answered the call,
for the sacrifices made
for liberty, justice
and freedom for all.
This is for those soldiers;
"we will remember the cost,
The ones who sacrificed
and the soldiers we lost."

Amanda Wright
*Bronson, FL*

*God is my inspiration in all things. My desire to write this poem came after I started thinking about soldiers, their families, and their sacrifices. I thought about the families always waiting, wondering, listening for a knock at the door. I wanted them to know they were appreciated. I wanted the soldiers to know that even though I am not on the front lines fighting with them, they are still in my heart and prayers. Their sacrifices have not gone by unnoticed. This poem was a way to say: thank you for fighting for me. I promise to always remember.*

## Our Creator

With a gentle touch
  of your finger,
You painted the
  beauty of the sky.
Adding just the right
  colors.
So pleasing to the eye,
  each unique white cloud.
Some with a silver lining
  took only one try.
Mountains in the background,
  some not quite so high.
Others almost blending right
  into the sky.

Jean Briscoe
*Hickory, NC*

*My name is Jean Briscoe, and I have dementia. My daughter Sharon is writing this for me. I have two other children, Kenneth and Julanne, and a wonderful husband Dean. I've been in a nursing home for over two years. I don't remember my family anymore, but they know I love them. I started writing poems years ago, and they're all about the Lord. My family found over eighty poems after I left home. This will be the second poem in a book, and I have two in a magazine, and I truly know my family is proud of me.*

## Untitled

Life is what you make it
Or so the poets say
To me I try to make the most
Of living every day
With a friendly smile, a kindly word
Can take a little time
But makes you feel it's worth it
And doesn't cost a dime

Dorenda Hubbard
*La Mesa, CA*

*We had been married for seventy-two years when my husband died recently. I continue to smile and greet residents and staff in assisted living and they always greet me back. This cheers me and helps to lower my sadness. Both British, my husband was a pilot during WWII and then became a test pilot earning one DFC and two AFCs. When he retired, we moved to California to work for Douglas Aircraft and later to Virginia. Our five grandchildren and four great-grandchildren live in Virginia. I'm now in California close to my daughter and husband.*

# Rainy Day Thinking

The light drizzle
Is a backdrop
A façade, an image
All a show, kind of like
A smile hiding
Teardrops
And it's funny, really
How alike
Teardrops and raindrops
Are.
They come with a storm
Relentless and heavy
Then
They start to let up
And in the aftermath
As eyes are dried,
Umbrellas closed,
Out comes the sun.
And it's funny, really
How alike
Smiles and sunshine
Are.

Alyssa Campbell
*Attleboro, MA*

## Go Tell

Jesus was born at Christmas
In the town of Bethlehem
In a lowly stable
There was no room in the inn

The angels proclaimed
Our Savior's birth
The Son of man
He came to earth

He picked some disciples
Fishing in the sea
With a simple command
"Come follow me"

We are commanded
To go tell all nations
Of the love of Jesus
He is our salvation

Praise Him! Praise Him!
Let your voices sing
Praise Him! Praise Him!
Our Lord and our King!

Jimmie Garrettson
*Smiths Station, AL*

# Stolen Dignity

My daughter met a girl, and brought her to my apartment;
This girl searched through each and every compartment;
Her goal was to rob me blind—
The lowest person you could find.
She acted too nice, and I knew something was wrong;
Now everyone tells me to be so very strong;
How can I do that, when my soul has been ripped out from the core?
What else is lurking, and will be in store?
She stole my jewelry, and money, too;
All I owned she took, and diligently went through;
My dad's diamond rings, she took away;
My mom's wedding band, and engagement ring, also came into play.
My uncle and grandfather's jewelry were taken too,
And so much more, but what can I do?
I have this sick feeling in my stomach which writhes in pain,
And I feel like I'll never come in, to get out of the rain.
My pride and dignity have all been taken;
My very core has been shaken;
Such a fate shouldn't be;
I ask, why has this happened to me?
Help me God to endure in the right way;
I feel like I'll be like this forever and a day;
Give me strength please, to get through this each and every day,
And for the answers I'll continually pray.

Marilyn Karter-Walicki
*Brooklyn, NY*

*I have had several poems published by Eber & Wein and am honored to have done so! I graduated from the Fashion Institute of Technology in Manhattan, NY. I was a textile stylist for a number of years. I've always loved and written poetry because I can share my feelings and perhaps touch someone, and make them feel good, on a particularly bad day. I love to help people! I am very emotional and write about things close to my heart. This poem was written out of despair and grief and is a true story about being robbed of all the possessions left to me by my family. The pain and heartbreak are indescribable, but I tried to truly depict my feelings! I have a wonderful husband William Walicki (Billy) a photographer, a daughter Alisa who excels in the fine arts, and a beautiful grandson Harley Lane who I truly believe will be someone you'll hear of, one day! He's four years old and is destined for fame!*

## Mom's Coffee

Mom's coffee is boring.
Her coffee is lame.
It's totally, absolutely, positively *not* my game!

Her coffee starts out black and hot.
I really think she could drink the whole pot.
Decaf it must be.
With a touch of sugar... it's as sweet as me!

Although it's totally, absolutely, positively not my game,
I still love her just the same!

Kensey Knight
*Kindred, ND*

*My name is Kensey Knight and I am nine years old. I have one brother, three step-brothers and three step-sisters. Most of the time, I live with my mommy, my brother and my step-dad in Kindred, ND, where it is very cold! I see my daddy too, who lives on a farm with our dog, Sadie. I enjoy reading, playing piano and guitar, sketching and writing. My inspiration to write this poem came to me while at the Starbucks drive-through with my mom. I love writing just as much as my mom loves her decaf non-fat with whip caramel mocha!*

# The Snowflake Family

Little hands, big hands and medium sized hands
No snowflake is exactly the same

I flutter down from the winter cold sky that covers a land of snow

My hands connect like a Lego
My arms link together like a family that loves the holidays
    and celebrating

We join in the center of gold and silver
We join like a chorus and sing Christmas songs
We sing like no one can hear us

When we join together we make a beautiful snowflake
One that isn't afraid to fall from the sky and seek
All the joys this world is really made of

Olivia Kugler
*Lincoln, NE*

*Olivia Kugler is twelve years old and lives in Lincoln, NE, with her mom, dad
and dog, Bo. When she isn't playing soccer or basketball, writing poems is her
passion. This poem was inspired by her family's favorite holiday, Christmas.*

## The First Snowfall of Winter

The first snowfall of winter is such a pretty sight,
It sparkles in the morning sun, and glistens in the night.

Each delicate creation that's made by God above,
Covers all the ground below, like a hand fits in a glove.

To each and every one of us, the snow means different things,
I think it all depends on age, what each emotion brings.

Snowflakes look like twinkling stars, as we gaze up to the sky,
Each one is soft and weightless, it's a miracle how they fly.

If you bundle up in clothing and stand stationary in one place,
You're warm and yet so very cold, as they melt upon your face.

There will be other snowfalls, but they won't mean the same,
As the first snowfall of winter, because you'll remember when it came.

So if you have to shovel it, or outside you get to play,
Enjoy the first snowfall of winter, before it melts away.

Sandra L. Button
*Great Bend, PA*

## Ancestors

the ancestors are talking
talking all the time to
anyone
who will listen

we get kind of busy
wrapped up in our
everyday lives and
everyday egos

so it's hard to hear
what the stones
are saying
hard to hear
whispered echoes

under
the
earth

the ancestors are talking
talking all the time
to anyone
who will listen

must wonder sometimes
what has
happened
to our ears

Matthew Loeterman
*Fair Oaks, CA*

*This poem was written over the course of a year spent in the desert. While enjoying clean air, an impeachable line of sight, often freezing, swallowing sand and tracking things that slither, pounce and fly, I wrote. I kept a journal, and another notebook for more whimsical expressions, for existential questions and idle ramblings. The universe asks me questions, and I feel for some response, inadequate though it may be.*

# The Family Tree: For Wynne

Immersed in the midst of our family's soul
We feel our own wings
Start to sprout and unfold
For around us we see
In magnificent array
The beauty of each one on display
Here a robin, there an eagle,
And a delightful wren
Each a charming specimen
Like a fine feathered friend
Perhaps a wise old owl
Or a grouchy jay
A grackle, or a mockingbird
All with their own special part to play
In the safety of this "nest"
We can try out our wings
We can practice the notes
Of the songs we'll sing
In each other we discover
A thousand tiny parts
Of who we ourselves are
Among common threads uniting our hearts
The babies, the youth and old alike
From swallow, to lark, to gentle dove
Find strength and shelter from the storm
In the comforting arms of our tree of love

Wynona Helfenbein
*Amarillo, TX*

*There is no easy way to describe the experience of being a little kid growing up in the middle of an extended family. There are moms and dads, brothers and sisters, grandmas and grandpas, aunts and uncles, and first, second and third cousins. Our best hope is to replicate it as closely as we can for the next generation. We were at our annual family reunion when my ten-year-old granddaughter, Wynne, asked me to write a poem for her; "The Family Tree" is Wynne's poem.*

# Lose Yourself

A day like today
People could lose themselves
Relaxing and kissing
Their worries good-bye.

The insects with mosquitoes
Being the den leader
Of all who hover and pester.

But on this day,
God gave all sun worshippers
A break from those flying nuisances.

Shadow and mist are not invited
To this fun affair.
But like taxes, it's all in
The cycle of life.

With laughter and love
The ingredients that
Surround this world
With smiles and butterfly whispers.

Kevin Lopez
*Broomfield, CO*

## Pondering

She just had to think about it.
She said, this is all about me, as she walked along the winding
  Path going nowhere in particular.
She wondered out loud if her life would ever be spectacular
  Or dull like some of her friends and one in particular.

Maybe she ought to tell that person she really doesn't know
  Where she is going
Maybe then they would feel differently about her, knowing.
  But then that could be best.

Did she want to spend her life with someone who may be aimless
  Even with desirable traits such as looks, manners and a soft caress
Even though scant interest in exploration, adventure and books?
  Then back again to manners and especially good looks.

If the best is yet to be perhaps a different path
  Or a sideways glance
Maybe at the library, church or the
  Community dance.

Then suppose there is no one who really fits the bill
Will she have thrown away her last chance?

I'll just have to think about it, said she.

Snake Freeman
*Port St. Lucie, FL*

*Snake Freeman, retired and living in Florida, saw combat in the Air Force during WWII. After graduating from the University of Virginia he moved to Washington, DC, to attend graduate school. He had two careers, one with the Department of Justice and the second with a large trade association. He wrote this poem after contemplating the plight of young people, including his grandson and granddaughters, as they made tough relationship decisions, some life changing.*

# Birth of Autumn

As I wandered down a shaded lane,
I saw that summer had gone again.
The trees they seemed to be a sighing,
For upon their branches the leaves were dying.
Colors splashed red, orange and brown,
As dry crisp leaves fell to the ground.
The death of summer green quickly came,
As the birth of autumn shaded the lane.

Melba Renard
*Escondido, CA*

# The Biggest Mistake

The biggest mistake
People make
Is deciding God doesn't exist…
And cross Him off their list!

Dolores Livingstone
*Fayette City, PA*

*I'm a seventy-six-year-old widow with two children, three grandchildren, and two great-grandchildren! God has blessed me greatly. About eight years ago, I was having prayer time and God said, "Write!" So, I took up my pen and wrote a beautiful poem! He's been giving me poems to write everyday since then, so needless to say, I have many poem books! I give "God's poetry" to people who need encouragement. I've never sold any of them. I feel they are a gift to me from God! Thank you for honoring poets like me!*

## Flame in the Wind

Life is suspended
Flame in the wind
Crystal snow alight with you
Tattered flakes fall in silent sadness.
Intensity of longing love burns
Life flashes like a flame in the wind.
How rare now the moment it leaps strongly.
Through ice blue pools of light
Your soul gazed naked upon mine.
Could all that was have never been
Could all this world in that one moment stand
Held by a gaze.
I play with the toys of life
Not to remember my vow.
I bleed with all that lives
What God's folly would create a soul
No body can bear
A weaver of dreams that none will share
A flame in the wind.

Clare M. Tonry
*Portsmouth, VA*

# The Grand Test

Your demons are at rest,
When they wake you are given a test.

Hello darling shall we go?
Your heart racing, your blade dragging slow.

Tear through your canvas made of skin,
Paint your emotions buried deep within.

Quite the artist you became,
This art you create is not so very sane.

Bleed out your pain now you are done,
Now that you've finished your world goes numb.

In the end your work is given a score,
Before you could read it you lay dead on the floor.

During this test you availed,
Sorry my dear you have failed.

Mya Kiles
*Fairfield, CA*

*This poem was written as a relation to my own personal life, for at the time and even now I struggle with coping in a healthy matter just as many others do. In all hopes I do wish this poem will speak out to someone who may be in the same situation as myself and realize that self harm and suicide is not the answer to a temporary problem.*

## Sonnet 1

There are whispers in my twilight
Of ancient ways, simple and profound
Hands shivering, I enter the burning night
Stepping softly on this place's solid ground
My mind runs, but my body will walk
Away from the shouts to find music
I listen to the singing-way the birds talk
And wonder how not to lose it
My thoughts follow the river, it leads
My breath follows the wind, it understands
I am apprentice to the crunching of the leaves:
No less delicate than any other plant
When sunrise comes the wise will speak with whispers
For there is beauty revealed by Earth's listeners

Caeley Kane
*Raleigh, NC*

*Caeley Aiden Kane is a graduate of UNC-Asheville. She also enjoys walking barefoot in summer, flipping through old books, sleeping until the afternoon, waking up for sunrise, and savoring good food. She believes that there is a lot to learn from observing and interacting with the natural world. (Her nature loving parents were probably a big influence in this!) A southern girl raised in Raleigh, North Carolina, she has now moved further south to Ecuador where she is working with a local sustainable development non-profit, EkoRural, on initiatives to increase access to healthy, local foods.*

# Intensive Care

Sadness you are to me.
Pain, suffering, a bitter wound hurt deep enough to
Bleed forever.
A cast of conflict internally needling at me.
Then you see me and smile, somewhat hospitably.

Joy you are to me.
Happiness, warmth, a sweet tender swab of sedation that
Heals the hurt
And makes me feel slightly recovered.
But the smile fades too quickly warding away my medicated hope.
My heart massages the pulsating feelings I still have for you
With a soothing salve of sympathy for myself.
Only faith nurses me back to a patient but critical state of love.

Distant you are to me.
Operating in your own world, corridors apart.
Bandaged with other concerns and feelings.
Your interests are steadfast and unconscious of my probing thoughts
Gloved with pure and sterile wishes for that perfect reciprocation.

Everything you are to me.
Pain in turn has induced the regret that you still aren't mine
permanently and
Privately, the treatment continues.
My soul is drugged with or without you, a tranquilizing truth.
Drowsily it whispers beneath the blankets of bleakness in a
Bed of hopelessness.
The original prognosis persists. My condition is malignant.

Karen P. Condeni
*Findlay, OH*

*I am an amateur writer who enjoys the creativity and expression of the arts in
general. I have been involved in education, both secondary and higher education, for
the past forty-one years. Also being a Midwestern wife, mother and grandmother,
my writing reflects the sensitivity and viewpoints of a full life and many relatable
experiences and thoughts. My poem submitted was based upon a relationship that
brought much joy and sorrow. It is reflective of how our unique human emotions
can render us truly vulnerable.*

## Winter Sunset

I saw it first as I turned west toward home…
  the early flames, hesitant, uncertain,
  licking at the edges of the deepening blue,
  tentative tongues of rose-crimson, pink-purple, gold-glint;
then, grown confident, they leaped across the sky:
fire out of control!

  Are there no sirens screaming the disaster to the town?
  No firemen, with set jaws, rushing to hose the flames away?
  No crowds, alarmed yet captivated, converging on the scene?

Against that willful blaze were opposed
  only slim stark sentinels, silhouetted in a straight line,
  stretching their leafless arms to contain the conflagration.
How useless their attempts; the flames would not be restrained.
  They oozed into puddles of icy water,
  sprang into west-staring windows,
  flowed into my soul.
What delight to be awash in that fiery flood!
My pyromaniac heart willed it to prevail.

It burned itself out, as all fires must, soon or late;
the flames subsided to embers, cooled to ashes,
  but heart-heat lingered long.

And yet again tonight, in my mind's eye,
that same fire flashes from an ashen sky.

Betty Schwartzhoff
*Caledonia, MN*

## Ode to Mom and Dad

We were blessed to have
parents that lived to be
in their eighties and nineties.
We were blessed by the
love they gave.
They were blessed by the
love they received.
Now, here we stand
on the final day in the house
that we all loved.
But, it's not the structure
that counts,
it's the love that lived
within these walls in the
name of Christ our Lord.

Edie Baker
*Council Bluffs, IA*

## How Is It, You Do Not Know?

How is it, you do not know?
How it is, I love you so?
Could I write it in the sand?
Could I gently squeeze your hand?
Could I write it in the sky,
among the clouds there, tethered high?
Could I carve it in a tree,
with my hands, on bended knee?
Could I tell you, how I dote,
on you, with pen and note?
Could I send a telegram?
But would you even know who I am?
How can I let you know,
how it is — I love you so?
Can I whisper in your ear,
that you're precious and so dear?
Can I voice it from my lips,
and lovingly kiss your fingertips?
Can I look into your eyes,
and ask the question, *why?*
*Why…* it is, you do not know,
How it is… I love you so?

Mary L. McKelvey
*Vinton, LA*

## Mama

My hands were busy through the day
But I saved a lot of time to play
The little games you asked me to.
I washed your clothes, I sewed and cooked
But when you brought your picture book
And asked me please to share your fun
I'd say, "Sure, I'd love to, Hon."
I'd tuck you in all safe at night
Read a little story, turn out the light,
Then tippy-toe softly to the door.
I longed to stay a minute more
'Cause life is short, the years rush past
A little child grows up too fast.
I feel you still are at my side
With confidences to confide.
The picture books are put away
But there are still life's games to play,
There are good-bye kisses and books to read
So I hope ole Mom still fills a need.
My hands, once busy, will always be
Doing the things that still are me.
I'm glad I found the time to do
The little things you asked me to.

Geneva Duer
*Longwood, FL*

# Just Say No

Juan called that morning and said, "Brother, will you catch my bull?"
  I replied as honest as I could, "Our day looks pretty full."
His bovine was in a pasture with no fence and he was in bad need.
  I felt sorry and told him we would bring a few of our steed.
He said, "Come down Schoolhouse Road and turn in by the old
Hix place."
  When the four of us rolled in, we saw contentment spread across
his face.
We jumped 'em out, mounted up, and commenced shakin' out a loop.
  There he stood on an ol' pond bank like a pigeon on his stoop.
It didn't take that ol' boy long to see just what was on our mind.
  After a quick glance away, empty tracks were all we could find.
My daughter and I did our best to try and pick up the trail.
  We caught a glimpse, as he jumped the fence, and all we saw was tail.
Clipped two strands of fence and made it through to see what we
could find.
  Thinkin', if I could only catch up, that ornery wretch is mine.
Busted into a clearing, his head up high, really Ballin' the Jack.
  My old horse got excited and it wasn't speed he did lack.
Closed the gap, hit a dip, cut a flip and on my back I lay.
  I was still, but my horse got up, and a ton of beef got away.
Moanin' and groanin' while trying to evaluate my plight.
  Daughter and Brother found me but when my eyes opened I'd lost
my sight.
I called for water from my saddle, which was brought without haste.
  Aimed for my mouth but it went in my nose and I never got a taste.
With all my strength they pulled me up and put me in my leather chair.
  A ½ or ¾ from the truck, the pain was all I could bear.
We rounded up my son who seemed to have missed the whole
blame show.
  Loaded up, headed home thinkin', "I should've just told Juan no!"

Brandon Yates
*Preston, MO*

*I was able to put into this poem the real life occurrences that I experienced while
helping a neighbor. Growing up on a small ranch catching wild cattle can be
fairly common while dying is not. My story was not embellished or exaggerated.
After telling my story over and over, I decided to put it into a poem. I regained my
sight after thirty minutes or so, underwent clavicle surgery and now will carry a
permanent reminder (a titanium plate and nine screws). I still help neighbors only
more cautiously; it's just my nature I guess.*

## Jesus Gives a Song

Anyone can sing
When the sun shines bright
But can we sing
When clouds turn black as night?
Anyone can sing
When all is right
But can we sing
When peace becomes fright?
Anyone can sing
When walking in the light
But can we sing
When we lose our sight?
Anyone can sing
When full of might
But can we sing
When strength takes flight?
Jesus gives a song
When in the night!
Jesus gives a song
When paralyzed by fright!
Jesus gives a song
When left with no sight!
Jesus gives a song
When weak lacking might!

Rhonda K. Evans
*Clarendon, TX*

*My dad was known for his singing voice. He and his siblings sang in gospel groups all of their lives. I would always stop whatever I was doing and listen to their music. It is a very deep and important part of my heritage. My dad and his siblings have all gone on, but their music and songs still live in my heart. Jesus is who gave all of us the song and talent to use for His honor and glory. God Bless!*

## The Resurrected Heart

I wrote a poem once to a friend to whom I was allured,
And now with caution at an end, I am annotating it again.

Surely anyone reviewing, might in conference declare,
Because of age a case of puppy-love, dupes this author debonair.

My bravura could be lessened, if in passing I had said,
"Just how exquisite her features were," I'm writing it instead.

Impressing one with words, that all should understand,
Just to please, yet still confirm, these excerpts from my hand.

Then soon it was, a faith's reward, she touched my eyes again,
And stepping back into my youth, I hastened to this pen.

Reflection in a transom with the sun traversing right,
Are cloud formations captioned underneath the straying light.

But, annexed to this backdrop, presides another name,
That takes the vision far beyond a comely windowpane.

Once in the store my cart is lured straight to where she clerks,
Where at the end my heart is moored, a queen disguised there lurks.

And so, when partiality erupts, encouraged to bestow,
The poem factory conjures up these words filled in below.

Dazzled by perfection, as close as I could tell,
Some symmetry of beauty, passed me by and cast its spell.

This must be where the master, playing clown and juggler too,
Enjoyed a bit of laughter, or maybe missed a cue!

*Go then!* Separate this time between, another hundred years.
I'd still extol these words to her, signed, Prince of Cavaliers.

John Cook
*Fresno, CA*

# Real Friend

What is a real friend to you?
Is it someone you can confide into?
Is it someone who's with you through thick and thin?
Someone who isn't there just when you win?
Someone you can depend on someone you can trust,
Someone who will be there when they must.
Who will always be a true friend in your eyes?
It's got to be one who won't fill your heart with lies.
One who's always loyal always there for you,
We're stuck in an age where loyalty's just a tattoo.
Loyalty means I'm with you wrong or right,
But I'll tell you when you're wrong and help you get it right.
A real friend will help you no matter what it may be,
And never stop to think about what's in it for me.
There's been people I thought I could trust with my life,
Since I've been down it feels like I've been stuck with a knife.
Take a good look at who you think is your real friend
Because when you hit rock bottom you'll realize most just pretend.

Matthew Luke
*Oakdale, CA*

## Satan's Water

I stopped at a party with my best friend,
wish I'd have known how this night was to end.
He appeared from a dark room filled up with smoke,
handed me something said, just take one toke,
it quenches your thirst just like water would do,
I put it to my lips without having a clue.
I looked all around me, just want to fit in
so I take my first hit and my head starts to spin.
He leaned into me said, that's heroin,
my greatest achievement, welcome to sin!

Satan's water… Satan's water, it quenches your thirst
till your head starts to burst,
there's always a second once you've tasted the first.

My days turned to weeks, my weeks into years
I lost all my family, my job and my cares.
Now all that matters this incredible thirst,
I need to keep drinking 'cause I'd tasted the first.
I've had so much now that my skin starts to crawl,
wish I had family just someone to call.
It's over for me now I have no more thirst;
I'm all alone now in the back of a hearse.
His water is strong makes you lose all control,
wish I'd stood up and just told him no.
I'm under the ground now I had to give in
don't take that first sip because Satan will win…

Jeanne Wolf
*Bloomingburg, NY*

## The Land of Forgetfulness

In the land of forgetfulness our mother went to stay
She didn't really want to but there was no other way

You don't go there to visit or knock upon the door
Once you enter you stay forever more

The days and nights are blended you can't tell spring or fall
It really doesn't matter you don't mark time at all

Kindness helps you travel down this trail of loneliness
Where every day seems to say how did I get in this mess

In time you can't remember your children or your friends
Or even your caretaker upon whom your life depends

Each day your mind wanders in places oft unknown
Searching for answers and longing for home

This road you have to travel by yourself it seems to me
Until the time you cross the line to eternity

Judy Rasmussen
*Twin Falls, ID*

*This poem came to mind as my husband's mom (my best friend) traveled from dementia to Alzheimer's. She and I decided at the very start of this relationship that we were going to learn to love one another: fifty-two years of laughing, crying, comforting and supporting each other through thick and thin. She was ninety-five years old when she took her last fall, broke her other hip and hit her head. This was the only time she did not know who I was. Mom died May 17, 2014; there is a hole in my heart where she lived.*

## The Fishing Trip

"I'm going fishing," the little boy said
As he grabbed his line and pole
He dug some worms down by the shed
And went to the old fishing hole
He went off gaily, the bliss of the young
His eyes untroubled and gay
His mother smiled at her little son
As he went fishing that day
Noontime passed, the sun went down
And still the lad was gone
His mother waited with a troubled frown
But the boy wasn't home by dawn
His father and friends all searched for him
They found his line and pole
They found the boy, he'd gone for a swim
And had drowned in the old fishing hole

Margaret Lent
*Longwood, FL*

## Our Moment

Our life is but a moment,
  The wise are heard to say,
For whether we live ten decades,
  Or just another day,

It is good for us to practice,
  To not live our moment in fear,
But with love and purpose and passion,
  Giving thanks each day each year.

It's an honor to have our moment,
  And it is given that we should use,
The talents granted to us,
  With a charge to not abuse.

The more seasons we have with our moment,
  The more mountains we are given to climb,
Till at last we will rest with those before us,
  In God's hands to the end of time.

So let's lovingly share our moment,
  With the people we meet each day,
Because we are all in this together,
  We're not on earth to stay.

Joe Chmura
*Antioch, CA*

*Poetry often reflects a very deep and intimate experience for the writer. It's one of the great tools we have as human beings to make rational sense of life's issues. The inspiration for "Our Moment" came after my dad passed away, then my brother, from cancer. When I reflected on their lives, I realized we are all stewards of our time. Our time can span a hundred years or be unexpectedly cut short. My hope is that you will embrace the beauty of each day, engage your talents for an honorable purpose, and lovingly share your moments with others.*

## Nature's Iterations

Gather up friends of feather,
Plan a route before bad weather,
Make use of earth's mysterious force,
Fly, fly the oft flown course.

Take note, short grow the days,
The winds blow cold, do not delay,
For soon the ground will be frozen,
You must begin the path prechosen.

Absorb the power of many a grain,
You will benefit from all you gain,
For ahead lies a journey long,
Draining the strength even of the strong.

And after months of time in the sun,
After cold winds and drifting snow have gone,
When icy flakes become warm drops of rain,
Take flight, take flight and fly back again.

Ken Frjelich
*Deerfield, WI*

# Choosing Paths

Life gives choices every day.
We walk paths not planned nor laid.
When we choose a path of change
Our lives are forever rearranged.

My daughter died at just twenty-one.
A family of three was now just one.
She left behind a little boy.
At three he loved his cars and toys.

As mother of a child now gone
I took the role for her as "mom."
This path I did not blink to take,
A choice one should not hesitate.

Many a night we could not sleep.
The pain for both of us ran deep.
Without him not sure where I'd be
A child's death changes you and me.

Life was hard starting again
He soon became my little man.
First days of school, holidays together,
We had each other no matter the weather.

The joy, however, has far outweighed
Any ups and downs had yesterday.
For I am where I am supposed to be.
I chose the path not planned you see.

Connie D. Lann
*Rancho Cordova, CA*

## Libby Dear

Where did you come from Libby, dear?
Out of the everywhere into here.

Into our hearts where love for you grows
Into the depths of our very souls.

Into our home like a ray of sunlight
Into our arms to hold you tight.

Into our minds to make memories of you
Into our feelings that will always be true.

Into our days to bring us cheer
Into our nights to calm your fears.

You came as on delicate gossamer wings
So we could teach you special things.

Kissed softly by angels up above
Sent by God with His special love.

Where did you come from, Libby dear?
Out of the everywhere into here.

Helen M. Townley
*Ewing, IL*

*I have been writing poetry since I was a teenager and I love reading it. My husband and I live in a small farming community in deep Southern IL. I wrote this poem for my granddaughter, Elizabeth Ashley better known as Libby, when she graduated from high school to place in her memory book.*

# A Thanksgiving Prayer

For all the blessings we received,
We thank you Lord today.
To You, we lift our hearts and eyes,
With gratitude we pray.
For all the beauty everywhere,
Created by Your hand.
It was done with love and gracefulness,
In this majestic land.
For the harvest, we are grateful Lord,
It shows Your loving care.
You've enriched our life so tenderly,
We know, You're always near.
For all these wondrous gifts from You,
We thank you, Lord above.
We offer our deep respect,
And our sincerest love.

Sonja Elko
*Red Bluff, CA*

## Take Me

Take me
For the fight is going out of me.
Take me
For I'm struggling to hold on.
Every breath I take
Becomes harder and harder.
Take me
To a place free of pain.
Take me
Where I can be happy again.
I'm fading fast
If anyone can hear me.
Take me
Where I can be me again.
Take me
To end my pain.
Life is leaving me
My family, I'm ready to die.
Take me
So peace I can find.
Take me
I am free!

Deb Alpaugh
*Turbotville, PA*

*My husband and I own a seventy-two-acre farm where we raise beef, hogs and goats. We enjoy pulling miniature horses. My poem, "Take Me," was written in memory of my father who passed away September 15, 2014, after a long battle with cancer. All he wanted was for his pain to end. His words stuck with me and "Take Me" was written to help his spirit find its freedom from the pain and suffering. This is for you, Dad! I love and miss you!*

## There Is Still Dawn

Understanding eludes me
Consumed by loss, filled with anger,
A pain from my soul has come forth.
My only response, why?
Then, in remembering I know.
There will never be more than I can bear.
Through the darkest forest there is still dawn.
From hopelessness, I can find strength,
And from the depths, I can see the lights of love.
The faces of those that depend on me.
Although I cannot understand why,
I know for all things there is a reason.
I must continue, of this I am sure.
There are many who still need me.
And yes, there is one who needs nothing.
Because in God's grace and loving embrace,
He is protected, strong, and home.

Mary Ann McKee
*Lexington, SC*

## A Promise

I'll fold your clothes
I'll brush your hair
I'll open your door
I'll carry your bags
I'll wash your dishes
I'll clean your house
I'll cook your dinner
I'll take you for late-night ice cream
I'll give you the last bite of crème brûlée
I'll tuck you in when you don't feel well
I'll hold your hand in public (everywhere!)
I will do all the little things
That matter most but get
Lost in a sea of "normality"
Unheralded
I promise to do them all
Evermore
Because the
Extraordinary
Makes for
Great stories;
The
Ordinary
Makes for
Wonderful lives...

Brett Nathan Humphreys
*San Francisco, CA*

## My Psalms 23

The Lord is my shepherd
I shall not want
That monster called depression
Trying to have me but don't
Keep showing your ugly face
And trying to stick around
Trying to make my home your place
But you about to get clowned
'Cause I'mma keep moving
And I'mma keep going
I'mma keep spitting
And I'mma keep flowing
Surely goodness and mercy
Shall follow me all the days of my life
So I'mma keep living
'Cause I'mma be alright

Justus Lederrick Clark
*Cedar Hill, TX*

## Never Alone

Everybody is living for today,
never thinking it might be taken away.
Everybody is scared to die,
nobody really knows why.

Where do I go from here,
friends seem to disappear.
How do I face tomorrow,
living in all this sorrow.

Tell me which path I should take,
keep me from making mistakes.
Help me to understand,
you will always lend a hand.

Tiffany Nicole Wise
*Victoria, TX*

# Life

Colorful stars gracing dark nights,
ravishing dawning day,
rising sun over the orient clouds,
blue and bright morning sky,
gentle breeze sweet and cool,
enchanting foliages and gorgeous flowers,
awesome plumages, exciting spots and stripes,
fetching rivers meandering through the earth,
magnificent lakes calm and comely,
blue, rolling and sightly seas;
undulating hills and magnificent mountains,
the human person full of splendor:
life is beautiful if only we can think.

Athanasius N. Okeiyi
*Pocahontas, AR*

*Athanasius N. Okeiyi is a Nigerian writer, musician, and social and environmental activist whose deep love for nature is reflected in most of his essays and poetry. The poem, "Life," is one of such numerous articulations of his inspired by nature. He lives and works in the United States of America.*

## Red

Red
The rich sugary juice of fresh
ripe strawberry is a drooling temptation of delight
and balmy happiness.

Red
Dark scarlet silk flowing freely
through the fresh air with the butterscotch sun
rising high above.

Red
The succulent bitter wine flowing
above your eyes reminds you of the beautiful
poppies growing in the field.

Red
Cherries the color of the red violet sky
after a brutal and everlasting
monsoon rain.

Red
The dark mysterious rain hot like
the flow of blood gushing
through your veins.

Aimee Ann Berry
*Phoenix, AZ*

# Scarred

Disaster, a catastrophe
Changing all lives
The young and the old
Hardships just ahead

Protests and marching
Wherever you go
Cold feeling filling your body
Tearing through like wildfire

Burn scars, yet
Nobody sees them
Hidden there, just beneath the surface
Hiding away to seem strong

People boarded out, boarded in
Caged wherever you go
Like a herd of wild animals

Suffering quietly without complaint

Emily Rose Brandon
*Depew, NY*

## Poetry

Poetry is such a marvelous topic
To write on poetry of expressions
Poetry with inspirational, motivational
On life, love, friendship, romance
Coming from an author such a
Tremendous gift of art love you not
Only for what you are, but for what
I am when I am with you poetry

Janessa J. Jordan-Rowell
*New York, NY*

*My name is Janessa Jordan-Rowell and I'm a self-published author. My book's website is www.lulu.com/spotlight/nessa212 and is also available on Barnes and Noble's website. I have a poetry blog at www.poeticus.com/janessa-jordan. I am also a shoe web designer at www.aliveshoes.com/appleness. Appleness is the shoe brand I created. What inspired me to write poetry is getting these ideas that I like to write on as feelings of inspiration. Writing helps me get stuff off of my brain and feelings I have onto paper. Some of my poetry is very deep and thoughtful. I wrote the poem on the topic of poetry, it represents it as it means to stand out strong. I love writing poetry and there is a lot of meaning in it.*

## Fishy Fishy

Fishy, fishy in the river,
does cold water make you shiver?
If pneumonia you do fear,
here's a plan for you my dear.
If my hook there you do bite,
and if it is you hold on tight,
there is a nice warm place I know,
where if you'd like we soon could go,
a place where I could cover you,
with lemon, onion, spices too,
and in tin foil you would snuggle,
and up this river no more struggle.
When that bright light you do see,
remember how 'twas nice of me,
to give you sweet a place to rest,
where no more upstream you must quest,
no more to fray fins on those rocks,
no more to dodge bears wanting talks,
no more to fight with other males,
who want to stroke your girlfriend's tails.
Yes, if it is you come with me,
what a great thing it will be.

Neil Douglas Carrell
*Tacoma, WA*

# Five Minutes a Day

Darkness prevails over Mideastern sands,
Gripping the hearts of all foreign lands.
Unconscionable, religious, political craze...
*"God save the children!"* the atheist prays.

It baffles the mind, an evil so cursed.
Warmongers conspire to fill up their purse.
What can we do? What can we pray?
Do we just turn and wait for judgement day?

What we don't want to know, it makes us all cringe,
It is time… to awaken the light from within.
Darkness and shadow, it's all a facade.
The war is with spirit measuring distance from God.

We created this evil just living our lives,
Wandering about electronically mesmerized.
If we all will just take five minutes a day,
Our love and our light will keep evil at bay.

Toni Riesen
*Portland, IN*

## Go Away

I'm not fit to be a mother,
My newborn baby needs to go.
I'd rather give him to another,
So I can keep snorting this blow.

Maybe I'll leave him on a doorstep,
Or forget him at a local store.
I don't care if I get a bad rep,
I'm already known as a whore.

Looking down at him, I see baggage,
He will only get in my way.
I refuse to push a baby carriage,
And listen to him scream all day.

I can't afford this baby, to feed,
Because his father is such a sleaze.
And my addiction to smoking weed,
Causes me to pay by on my knees.

So how do I get rid of this child?
I don't want him in my life.
My single lifestyle is way too wild,
He needs a husband and a wife.

Corissa Beck
*Overland Park, KS*

*At age twenty-four, as a combat war veteran for the US Army, I have seen many horrific things. Nothing compares, however, to the problem of abandoned children in the world today. This epidemic was my inspiration for this poem. This will be my second published poem, and my goal is to express, through words, the importance of a young, innocent life.*

## Beautiful Black Girl

Beautiful black girl with the natural mean face.
Bestowed with trials and tribulations
of her inherited disadvantaged race.
With a taste of disgrace when she walks into a place.
Death to her own voice, so her percussion rises amongst others.
Beaten and loved by the black and white brothers.
Groomed to grow up in the way of their mothers,
constantly penalized because she is different from others.
Soft skin, cold heart, thick legs, set her apart.

Beautiful black girl born into this world longing for greatness
to take her places.
Her yacky curly hair, and if she loves it, we'll that's rare.
To love her man with such care,
to have her heart, and her underwear.
Precious smile to cover her fears,
precious fingers to wipe her tears.
Blessed child that is a temple,
withstand the break, to transform into a dimple.
Rage like fire, love like the sea.

Beautiful black girl born to be.

Jamayrah Elizabeth Moore
*Trenton, NJ*

*I wasn't inspired to write this poem, I was obligated. I was obligated as a young
African American woman to write this poem to let the public know the truth.*

## Tomato Love Easter Monday

Snaking through the back field
blanketed with ivy and sassafras
avoiding angels in August
in the God-drenched air.

I have left you in charge
of my progeny
staked-tomato plants
yellow flowers bursting.

We circumnavigate the United States
leaving you alone
to earn the daily bread.

Yet you always water my Big Boy tomatoes
surprising me on the family's return
with their height and bounty.

The sassafras makes great tea
after extracting the tap root
wild strawberries grow.

But your love mingles with the soil
your patience waters my plants
and the tomatoes burst with juice.

Anne Croly
*Bronx, NY*

## Tainted Vitality

His beastly excitement over the word *"no"*
Has been thrust inside her repeatedly.
Warmth escapes her heart, while he ravages his prey.
Trickling tears mix with hot blood
As her words are slain in the depths of her throat.
Purity tainted by the stench of alcohol and regret.

A zombie-like trance is induced
As the life slowly pours out of her.
The only escape in this terrifying moment
Is to bore him with her motionless body.
This goes unnoticed by the dreadful creature
And he continues to coat the victim
In his foul breath and saliva.
He seems to inhale her life as his climax
Approaches and she continues to drain.
The monster explodes with dominant force,
Sealing his conquest and expelling his venom.
He embraces the motionless body,
As he pollutes her with his vile being.

He slithers off her porcelain skin
And takes a long look at his victim's carcass.
Faint breath, lifeless eyes: just the way he dreamed.
Another angel loses a part of her vitality,
So that the demon may feel his.

Kelly Stillufsen
*Manorville, NY*

## October Time

May the leaves start falling in all their grace,
While a jack-o'-lantern smiles at you with a spooky face,
Skeletons dance and bats do fly,
It's October time, me oh my.

As the witch cackles stirring her magical brew,
The autumn fall wind will sing to you,
Apples, pumpkins, and Ichabod Crane,
Cider, squash, and a headless horseman with no name.

Halloween's eve is soon on its way,
Listen to the wolf howl that mystical day,
Dracula is ready and his night is soon to be here,
Light the black candle and watch the witches appear.

Trick or treat is the game the children play,
Bags of candy are their hope for the day,
The moon is full with a yellow glow,
Company is coming, oh my, it's time to go.

Enjoy the season and the time to be had,
Don't forget to be good and not bad,
Why you say, it's odd I ask?
Remember he wears a red suit not a mask!

Debra Hrynyk Nelson
*Phoenix, AZ*

## The Indians on the Hill

So many things remind me of
The Indians on the hill
When I see the tall grass growing
Blowing from side to side
Moving from the power of the mighty wind
I can see the Indians carrying their baskets
Made from the straw that the grass gives
Their women are weaving beautiful baskets
Their children are playing on the hill
The men are dancing and singing
I can see their painted horses
So strong and so beautiful
They have such great joy
Big happiness
For the love of the land
The thrill of the hunt
The great trees on the hill give shade
To shelter from the mighty sun god
The power of the sun is magical
Growing plants, animals, and man alike
Glistening off of the beautiful streams
The streams flowing giving the same life

When I look on the hill

The Indians on the hill

Are no more.

Tony Moran Burgos
*Stockton, CA*

# Opioid Epidemic

Human lives cursed with affliction
Among the worst: addiction.
Cannabis not always happy,
Weed grow all over map-py.

Nicotine, cigarettes, and alcohol all bad,
But coke and dope make minds go mad.
Theft here, stealing there,
Drug money asks: a dime to spare?

Ride high, and opium becomes opprobrium.
Percs and oxys come with constipation ad nauseam.
Afghan poppy crop makes big money from a lot.
Heroin injected ends with a body shot.

Brains, liver, bones, lives lost to dope.
Mothers' tears and loved ones left to mope.
Land of the free, home of the brave,
Daily dope is life like a slave.

Lives and souls slave to drug,
Human families drop like a slug.
Here today, gone tomorrow,
Each overdose a legacy of sorrow.

Plant not poppy but seeds of hope.
Joy and fulfillment in a life free of dope.
On Flanders Fields let poppies grow;
Take no harvest for a better tomorrow.

Katherine Murray Leisure MD
*Plymouth, MA*

## Housewife Lament

Robins dart avoiding fate.
Feline reality it arrived too late.
Toddler reach, a wayward ball.
Inapt balance, resulted fall.
A spectator of others' adventures.
Fear mine will never start.
Blessed to be a mother.
The mundane will surely smother.
Hopes and dreams, from forgotten past.
Replaced by a smiling mask.
You are so lucky, people say.
Don't have to work, just play all day.
Grass is not greener on this side.
The field of lonely, where I reside.
Yellow and brittle boredom turns.
Once vibrant hue melancholy burns.
The fire that once blazed within.

Glenda Elaine Nickell
*Austin, TX*

## The Dream

Wheels screeching,
barely making the curve,
skimming the edge.
"Slow down," they call,
paying no heed to their worries.
Lapping 1, 2, 3… 4 people,
seeing the next,
seething with excitement.
Revving the engine.
Boom!
The jolt of crashing into the cart,
it veers off the course,
colliding with the barrier,
the driver scrambles off the circuit.
Crossing the white and black checkered line.
Oh!
The glories of being first.
Waking with satisfaction,
was it all a reverie?
The memory fading,
*no!*
Searching trying to get it back,
clawing through all of my thoughts and ideas.
It disappears in the light of day,
only to come back in the amenity and serenity,
of a moonlit night.

Alan Andrew Ngouenet
*Medina, WA*

## The Woman in Black

The woman in black is so venomous! *Whack!*
Spreads poison with her tongue
Leaves the unexpected stung
She lures victims in
To an entangled laced sweet
Disables heroes unsung with no chance for fleet
The woman in black is so poisonous *whack!*
Has a dark soul even darker than coal
She is treacherous, tricky, a two-timing troll
Hurt and humiliation—her ultimate goals.
The woman in black has a very bad track
While she stabs at your back with an ominous *whack!*
The woman in black should stay away from me *whack!*
And, woman in black—don't you ever come back!

Dora Elia Gonzalez
*Harlingen, TX*

# Monk

Time wants me at a high place
looking back on the path
I took to get there.
It will never come —
that belly-full of hours
where faith in my
memory of yesterday
whispers particles
that may or may not
exist in reality. I've chosen
to capitulate to hours
spent listening to the prose
and prayers of the wind
on empty mountaintops.
My body lies there now,
feeding carrion birds
that take me home one
moment at a time. Only
prayer flags flutter.

Michael C. Medler
*Mukilteo, WA*

*Words are pigment-laden brushes that, when spread with care, color our world. The emotions they evoke enrich us, lift us, become the breath that drives the cogent hammer that beats within us all. My goal is to drive that hammer.*

## Obesity

I love you.
You're always there.

I have no need to look for you. Solid, yet yielding
you protect me from harm and you nourish me.
You have no feelings, nor trust.
But I trust you.
I must because I've used you these many, many years.

And when some dolt criticizes you,
I defend you, comfort you,
feed you and cradle you.
You who are the closest friend I have.

I hate you! You restrict me, limit me, embarrass me.
I, wrapped in your warmth, shouldn't feel any pain.
Yet I cry from the pain you cause me.
The agony, the shame.

How I hate you
and love you.
And despise me
for staying with you.

Irene Paulette Silvey
*Pittsburg, CA*

## This Earth

To praise the paranormal earth,
remember the rich raspberries
on that delectable August afternoon.
The abandoned shed,
the weeds which constantly overgrow.
A pitcher of water
shattered on cement.
Appreciate this inconsistent earth.
Many walk the paths
those refugees walked.
The sunken ship
knows less neglect
than this abandoned earth.
A water bottle in the valley
that no one bothered to pick up
cupid's heart
imprinted in the battle scarred tree
a gunshot ruins
a hopscotch game
a perfect earth
is no earth.

Natalie Vargas Nedvetsky
*Wilmette, IL*

## Love Is Scary

Boy of my dreams
What a nightmare you turned out to be
I am happier alone than I ever am with you
But I cannot stand a moment without you
It's almost like I can't breathe when you're not around
But I am suffocating whenever I'm with you
You put me down in every way
But I know it's only because you care
I feel like you put a curse on me, to make me hate myself
But then a kiss breaks the spell, and I know that means I love you
I found out that you've been cheating on me
But I know that you love me, so I forgive you
You said you only did it because I'm not good enough for you
I'll try harder to make myself beautiful for you, whatever the cost
Even if it means going against everything I believe in
You told me I'm too fat
I said I would starve myself
You said that was a good idea
Oh my sweet love, I would do anything for you
I was talking to a man the other day
You thought I was flirting with the man, so you beat me
I am only allowed to talk to you, no one else
But you're all I'll ever need
Some people think we shouldn't be together
I feel bad for them
They just don't know what true love is

Maya Olivia Arroyo
*Strongsville, OH*

## Memory

To see beyond the memorial,
And view the life of those lost.
To see the pain of through their eyes,
And feel what they feel.
The pain, the sorrow, the loss of a brother,
And know that it can't be changed.
All just beyond a memory.

Anthony John Nunally
*Vinton, LA*

## I Can No Longer

I love you but I
can no longer be your everything. You
are powerful, smart, beautiful and yet somehow lost, in de-
nial. Apathy and depressio-
n your cage. Emotional certainty, an
outcome never realized. Grow up! I ye-
ll, but regret it instantly. H-
ow can I help? I can't, an i-
nconvenient truth. I let
go, but I'm scared. I can no long-
er be your everything. F-
reedom lies in you, not me.

Paul Eric Carey
*Port Moody, BC*

## Mirror's Age

As morn braces against the emptiness of night
And cock crows echo in waves of yellow light

Fallen mixed colors brush along the coarseness of stone
As fall would have them, these leaves of gold

Age as time moving swiftly through coveted hope
Laid far along twisted roads, yearning there and then
To be not parted here, have alas a distance near

But what of it, who so best to have it, more!

I tire now on thinking further,
And would love to simply settle
On piles of leaves bright along the way
To answer no more
To things that must stay

'Cause with any wisdom here,
I would have experienced it there
On piles of leaves I will stay, and rest a time
Before another day

And should it be the last of things, then so be it,
For I would have had what it was before its last,
And what more can I ask, to take on roads we cannot stand

Abel Olivencia
*Middle, NY*

# Yet

Have you noticed it yet?
Has it touched you yet?
Do you know what it is?
The abandonment of forgotten realities
And alternate universes you tried so hard to create
Have you noticed it yet?
That long stretched out road
Covered in your dirt
Blanketed in your failures
That's been stepped on by imitators
And mocked by the naive
Is that the remains of what you created?
Has it touched you yet?
That realization of the fact that the dirt you left behind
Can never be touched again
And is looked upon as
"Stupid"
Or
"Wrong"
Are you wrong for living the way you did?
Or
Are you wrong on the impression you left behind?
What is more important to you?
Do you know what it is?

Jonathan Ronald Chesbro
*Peabody, MA*

# A Cutter's Diary

He had tattoos on his back,
Locks on his head,
Hate in his heart,
Me in his bed.
His eyes were brown.
He reminded me of you.
He had a mischievous grin,
A past filled with sin.
In one day he took me places I've never been.
He had scars on his back,
A flat top on his head,
And in his heart was love instead.
He was the opposite of you.
He had a perfect smile, filled with joy,
And a past he dares to remember.
He had curls on his head,
A smile that was dead,
My voice in his head.
He was the most beautiful thing I've ever seen,
Eyes green,
A mind that didn't fear to dream,
And lips that never told a lie.
Who is this he I speak of, could this he be all three?
Or is this he really a she?
Could this he I speak of be me?
You'll probably never know.
He was perfect, but he doesn't exist.
He is he who I wish to one day kiss, I wish to one day hold.
He is he who my heart will thaw out for, it will no longer be cold.
He is he who I'll become one with, combination of souls.
He is he who I'll one day grow old with.

He is all in my head.

Wendy Mybell Napoleon
*Brockton, MA*

# The Aesthetic of Deception

Her ashen face,
He caressed.
Eyes closed.
Raw desire overcame her.
With reflection,
She drew away.
Hands swallowed her.
A whispered cry
Chirped from beneath his grip.
Tears began to flow.
A reassuring smile
Painted across his lips.
Darkness.
Her body
Limp.

Ariel Landry
*Metairie, LA*

## T'lam Cemetery

*I am James Van Loon,*
*    Gone since nineteen-twenty-three...*

I remember this area,
this is where Dirk and I would have adventures.
The woods were our kingdom
and we both ruled the entire area together.
We would cause a raucous late into the night
after playing all day without rest
but now, now we rest in a new kingdom.
These woods, now gone, have been replaced by graves.
Here I rest in the afterlife with
my brother, my father, my mother and
three months from now the only sounds to be heard
are the wind in the trees
the crackling of ice below
and the soft chatter of tears above.
The fresh snowfall blankets our kingdom.
The colors of fall, vanished, and
nothing left but the white sheet
to protect us. A cutting wind blows from the west
chilling the mourners.
We cannot feel what they feel
see what they see
hear what they hear.
We no longer feel the late summer sun
the sounds of the peaceful breeze

or the twaddle in the trees.

Jake Klopfenstein
*Urbandale, IA*

# The World May Never Know

My days feel short, the years have gone fast,
I live in the present carved by my past.

As we float on, the seconds tick,
In Nature I find beauty, beauty that will slip.

In a world of no permanence, does it matter at all?
We are born to rise, we rise to fall.

All these thoughts, all these lies, they soon will pass,
If my being is infinite, why will my presence not last?

We face forward on our journey, through force and will,
We fill our glass full, only to spill.

A bittersweet song, the undeniable end,
When we leave, will our mistakes amend?

All the answers I desire, I will never receive,
Until the moment when, I too, shall be free.

All the knowledge of truths, irrelevant, at any rate.
Possession of answers does not distract fate.

Jillian Grace Usher
*Lake Havasu City, AZ*

## Nope to Dope

Since when is it normal for all of these teens,
To be pressuring their friends to smoke the greens,
You have too much work you need to do, you can't afford to crash
Just remember that when you're thinking about smokin' hash
Why do you feel the need to smoke dope
All I have to say is I have a little more hope
For my future, for this world, I want to make a change
I can't do that if I'm trippin' on something unproductive and strange
I mean I get it you think you're cool, yeah you're so fye
But tell me is it really worth it, getting super high
Like I'm sorry but you look like nothing other than a fool,
Talking bout being hipster, yup you're so cool,
Here's an idea follow the laws, there is a reason it's a rule
Otherwise you're going to look like nothing other than a tool
I really don't need to waste my hard earned money on a nug
When I can go see my friends and have fun without a drug
Personally, I'd rather be out active and getting toned,
Than sitting on my couch eating Cheetos and getting stoned
But really please tell me if it is worth it smokin' pot
When at every deal there is a chance of you being shot
For one little herb you're putting your whole life in danger
But even more, putting it in the hands of a stranger
So while you're begging me to join you and hit your little bong
I'm going to put my foot down, no matter what, I'm standing strong
Go ahead and make fun of me, call me boring and plain
But anytime you ask, I'll say no to Mary Jane

Regan E. McGovern
*Roswell, GA*

## Dreams

Dreams are dreams
Will they come true?
Maybe or maybe not
But if they do come true
Hold on type to that dream
And dream another dream

Sandy Holland
*Maben, MS*

## Listen

When apples fall down
and the world spins 'round
we all quiet down
and listen
to the beautiful harmonies
that the world around creates
we listen
to the crisp snap of a twig on the ground
and the beautiful bird calls that fill the air
we listen
to the sounds
of nature

Hayden Hall
*Darien, CT*

## Eternity

Someday, the coffee will not smell as sweet,
the laughter won't come as easily… tears will.
Life is not fair, but you got lucky… very lucky.
Not everyone experiences that kind of love.
Although the physical body has disappeared,
you have cherished all the moments.
Like her hand brushing your back as she slips into bed.
Close your eyes now. Hear the laughter? The song, your song?
Your soul mate is there, waiting until it's your turn.
I've heard this term so often, but what does it mean?

A soul mate touches more than your skin, they get under it.
They share the news of the day, and all of their heart.
Like the sole on a shoe, they are bound together.
They share the warmth of the sun and the starlight in the night sky.
They are free flowing music, rhythmic and dynamic,
filling the space between heaven and earth.
They do not understand "loneliness,"
They only know the feeling of "wholeness."

You were meant to stay behind and live a full life.
Know that someday, you and your soul mate will share eternity.

Kathleen M. Schuetz
*Mankato, MN*

# Legends

All great stories must end
One by one they vanish
Fallen through the fabric
Of space and time,
Never to be forgotten,
Never to be remembered,
Such is the plight of the legends
As time goes by,
Generations upon generations
Stories are forgotten
Legends fade into the woodwork
Never to be told,
Truths diminish with the years
As humans grow older
The lies grow bolder
And soon all that will be
Are the inaccuracies that you told me
So long ago
I doubt anyone would know
About the sadness
And the pain
And the sting of the end of a story
And the end of a world

Katherine Lorena Maynard
*Columbia, MO*

# When She Comes to Visit

when she comes to visit
everything changes
hide my things
clean my room
family stressed
sometimes I leave

when she comes to visit
we're happy to see her
she's been gone a while
but it gets old quick

when she comes to visit
she takes my bed
wrecks my room
and practically
shoots for my head

when she comes to visit
I might go crazy
the stress
the mess
the long nights
she's so crazy

when she comes to visit
it may be crazy
but when she leaves again
we all can't wait
for her to visit again

Madison Ruthann Orth
*Burlington, IA*

## Elysian Fields

Dreamt golden fields set me free
Place only gods are permitted to be
Ran down the aisles
Spinning around
Stood in the middle, heard no sound
Life flowed inside me, free
Happiness ran through my veins, ecstasy
Wind blew hard, everything started to sway
Persuaded, lifted my arms to praise
Wind blew through me, like it knew me
Caressed my skin, touched within
Revered
Worry disappeared
Elysian Fields
Never forgotten, deeply missed
Glorious, freedom and bliss

Dana Bradshaw
*Cypress, TX*

*I imagined a peaceful place located nowhere on land and far beyond the sea. The holy convocation was where flesh and spirit part ways, where all living things are set free.*

# Fri-ends

You, me
Right, left

So simple,
We two,
Walking in step,
In peace.

You, me
Right, left

I stumbled,
And you,
Thinking it best,
Walked on.

You were right,
I was left.

Alice May Lemieux
*Berkeley, CA*

# My Bewitching Opera

I sit in the moonlight surrounded by God's smallest gifts.

The foghorn echoes across dark water.

My heart beats rhythmically to its tempo.

Lights fight through dense fog. They are the lights of dreams
that only those who love the sea can conjure in their minds.

My boat gently rocks me, we have bonded a friendship
unlike any other. She offers comfort and I gaze in awe.
Her mast is tall and proud.
I am inspired to match her prowess.

We are meant to share this moment. We become one as I sit
in her old and defiant cockpit. Her greatness cannot be
denied.

I see the moon. It is the challenging the thick mist
and defeating its foe.

The fog has been bested and I witness the sparkling of dreams
dancing bravely across the water like an exquisite ballet.
The rumble of the foghorn is the finale of this bewitching opera.

The curtain has closed and I retire in peace.

Erin Nolte
*San Juan Capistrano, CA*

## Crazy Love

It's crazy how the ones you love the most
Are the ones who leave you in pain
God gives his reasons
With no words to explain.

Everyone can say they know
But truly they have no clue
It's the ones who say no words
Who have done through the same as you!

They know how it feels
To get your heart shattered to pieces
That's why they try not to remember
'Cause they feel it increases!

It's likely to say you don't care
And it's likely to say you hate
But once you fall in love
It's entirely too late!

You know deep inside
You wish things were still the same
Even after what they did
You just can't take the pain!

It feels like everything is wrong
And nothing will ever work out
But I promise in the end
You'll see what love's about!

Latifah Williams
*Houston, TX*

*I'm twenty-two years old. I'm a full-time student at the College of Healthcare Profession. I'm getting my degree in the medical assistant field. I'm a first time mom to a baby girl. She will be one year old on December 27, 2014. My family is my everything to me. My mother has been there for me since day one. I love my mom. Me and my mother moved from AZ to TX almost three years ago. We've been here in TX since 2011. I wrote this poem about my daughter and the guy that I'm dating right now. I feel crazy in love with the both of them from the bottom of my heart. When I first held my daughter, I knew I was going to love her forever. She is my first child and my everything. I love writing poems. I have a whole binder full of poems that I wrote myself. One day I'll get all my poems published in a book.*

## Sweaty Love

We were both shy, but him more so.
In the movies we would sit side by side,
His arm glued to the armrest and unmoving.
I wanted to reach for his hand
But my palms were hot and sweaty with nervous feelings
I thought, if only he'd reach for me;
If he wanted to, he could put his arm around me.
But his arm just sat there, still.

I wasn't watching the movie;
My mind was too busy thinking about touching his hand.
Time had passed, and my hands were less hot and sweaty now
Because I had been airing them out beneath the seat...
Maybe I should —

I went for it, impulsively touching his hand
And sending a flirtatious smile his way.
It was dark in the theater, but I could tell that
He was blushing.
And for the last ten minutes of the movie our hands intertwined,
Sweaty and sticky
Together.

Emily Holmes
*Boulder Creek, CA*

## A Glimmer of Wonder

When there's light we smile.
When there's sun we shine.
But there's so many wonders,
and such a shrivel of time.

The light may make us smile.
The dark may fade our shine.
But those questions leaving us wondering,
are those small thoughts left behind.

I've wondered, dreamed, and cried.
I've put light in every thought.
But every peace of light I miss,
is the glimmer I never brought.

Julia Lauren Smith
*Wellsboro, PA*

# Virus

Flow virus flow, the deadliest weapon ever go virus go,
but keep this pain of mine on the low virus low.

I know virus I know, the visions of her they come and go
come and go, it's your job so flow virus flow.

This feeling inside me is like steam it blows virus blows,
I love this what you have given me so go virus go,
this thing you call love it flows virus flows.

No virus no, I want more I like this feeling give more
give more, all day and night let it take over so virus so.

Feed virus feed, it feels good to me and her we never
want it to stop greed virus greed.

Yes, flow virus flow, you and her are all I want
in this world so flow virus flow.

Terrance Itego Tanner Jr.
*Jacksonville, NC*

*Like many of my poems, "Virus" started as a title. Once I write the title the rest just comes easy. I wanted to describe love as something contagious and deadly, and the first thing that popped up was a virus. This wouldn't be possible without God, my mother, Monique Latimer, my family that has supported me since the beginning, and the great Jessica Sutton who loves all my poetry. I pray you enjoy "Virus" and the others that follow.*

## They Call to Him

He spots their roundness yards away.
Whatever else he sees, I cannot say
but anyway, his gift dismays me.
He sees cold hard cash. He is one with them.
Yes. He detects coinage in all
their calibrated hiding places,
playing peek-a-boo in the grasses,
sleeping along the edge of the road, nestled
amongst the fallen leaves,
peeping from the concrete lip
of the sidewalk as we stroll hand in hand.
He sees each and every one.
They call to him, ringing out their round sound.
Summoning, beckoning—exclaiming their presence. Pick me!
Pick me! They shout to him.
As a homing pigeon, he spies their curvature
of green or darkest brown,
the coins not one other person has found.
They signal and he hears their ballooned sphere,
hollow and muted, yet distinctively there.
He picks them up, caresses their continuity
         …and gives them all to me.

Annette Jane Gagliardi
*Minneapolis, MN*

*My husband finds money wherever we go. Nearly everyday he places a penny, dime or other coin in front of me. Sometimes there is only one penny, other days even twenty-five or more cents worth of coins are displayed. "They called to me," he smiles in explanation. We can walk the same streets, the same parking lots and hallways and he will find the coins others do not. When our two youngest daughters took walks with us around the neighborhood, my husband would instruct them to look for pennies. Often, the girls would spy coins and delightedly exclaim over their find. Little did they know that their dad was dropping pennies from his pocket so they would be sure to come home with their "coinage."*

## The Red Deer

The red deer moos, growls, screams

His horns pressed to his withers as his head tilts back,
  so to be heard by all.

He screams of urgency, of panic,
  and of things he does not fully understand.

The old large buck looks over his harem
  as not to let one escape.

His son of last year, or the year before, waits just outside,
  on a hill close by.

He feels the urgency too,
  but knows the older stag will kill him if he trespasses.

His time will come, but not this year.

I dip my staff into the soft dirt and head onto the path,
  and trek up the winding forest trail,
  smiling, with the memories of younger years.

Donald Hamilton
*Bonita, CA*

# Nightmare

I couldn't find you,
In my dream from last night,
Oh what a scary thought,
To be lost in an unknown place,
And be frantically alone.

I searched and searched,
To find those brown eyes,
To see that contagious smile,
But all I would witness,
Was a missing piece,
In such a crowded place.

But as I woke,
Your arm around me,
My breathing slowed,
And I hoped to stay,
In this familiar place,
I'd like to call home.

Melissa Ann Barry
*Colchester, VT*

## Simple and Not Simple

My sadness does not weigh much.
My sadness is my own.
My sadness sits inside my chest,
it makes me feel I've grown.
Sometimes it travels up my throat
to tell me I'm alive.
Sometimes it bubbles over though
I don't always know why.
Your name, your meaning trigger it,
so does the evening news.
My sadness does not let me forget
that there are things to lose.
Here rests my smile near my tears
all mingled and confused—
cannot say it, can't convey it
but I keep taking its abuse.
My sadness will not leave me
and I don't want it to—

without it I might not know
there ever was a you.

Kara Rozansky
*Long Beach, NY*

## Fears

We break in tears from all our fears
Our thoughts are the ones that knock us off
We hide in our covers away from what hovers
For those who do uncover discover
That our fears come from within

Shirleen Maria Groves
*Pembroke Pines, FL*

## Ponderings in the Night

Down by the water in the dead of night
Beneath the stars and the dull moonlight
A young man stands down by the shore
As he has done many times before
And as he gazes at the stars out yonder
Once again he starts to ponder
Of what he is thinking no one can tell
It could be about life, death, heaven or hell
And while he stands gazing at the sky
He starts to smile, not knowing why
The reason he comes here I do not know
But I think it may be for inspiration and hope

Garrin Andrew Loveland
*Austin, MN*

# Different Seasons

Sometimes things just won't go your way,
But take out time to thank God for another day

God gives his people different seasons,
Whoever thought this would've happened for whatever the reasons

God didn't promise that things would stay the same,
Your season is up and now it's time for a new change

Don't look at the present or the past,
You will only hurt because of whatever happened last

Look to the future and see what it may bring,
Put God first and you'll get the very best thing

Whatever you're going through may seem like a curse,
Remember someone else is in your shoes or even worse

All you have to do is hold on and pray,
Now watch God work and take all the pain away

Sheena Tillis
*Tulsa, OK*

## The Memories

The hot air touches me like the sun shines through
The window
The wind blowing my hair through the glimmering sunshine
While I was playing through my memories
Thinking and waiting, that's when I notice
The hot colorful sun sat there waiting for me to run, dance
Outside in the blistering of the day
But I just sat there thinking, thinking of him
How he always tucked me in, every night
Kissed my forehead when he held me in his arms
Help him wash his trucks in the boiling, bright days
The red shiny trucks like a bright waxed shiny apple
Oh how I miss all of the memories
The washing, the kissing, the tucking in
All of those memories gone and nowhere to be seen, anymore
Just like the wind blew all of that away
And I just stood there watching it happen like I couldn't do
Anything, just stood there frozen
Fades away one sweet moment at a time
Into the darkness, that holds mysteries
How much I wish he was here holding me in his arms again
Him waiting for me when I got home
To swing me around like he used to
He was, and always will be, my
Number one
Dad.

Alyssa M. Slowiak
*Eau Claire, WI*

## Sisters Strengthening Sisters

Sisters strengthening sisters is what God called each of us to do,
Yet we allow circumstances, emotions,
And sometimes we ourselves from seeing it through.
We have all been charged to lift up one to the other and encourage,
Yet if the truth be told, instead we tend to discourage.
But today is a brand new day full of Gods' love, mercy and grace,
And together we can take what God has given us
And put a smile on another sister's face.
God's grace is sufficient and His love is pure and true,
My sisters if we say we trust Him then there is nothing we can't do,
This means no more excuses for not giving our best,
Just try Him and watch while He does the rest.
For on that solid rock we shall all stand,
Sisters strengthening sisters as we hold each other's hand.
To love always especially when we think a sister is unlovable to us,
Remembering just what Jesus did for us without even a fuss.
So let us start right now with open hearts and just listen,
We are supposed to be like Him, Christ-like, a Christian.
So as we walk this day forward by faith and not by sight,
We will be sisters strengthening sisters and doing it right.

Jeanne Ann Coward
*Brockton, MA*

*I have been writing since the eighties. I have written several books which include children's books and spiritual books of situations and circumstances that have happened in my life, along with over a hundred poems. My work has not been published but has been copyrighted. My poems are inspired by God and my love for Jesus Christ. My poems are used to encourage and lift the spirits of people. I pray that I have used my gift the best way I can and that I will be able to continue to do so as long as I have breath in me.*

## Last Moments of Her Life

Lost in utter confusion,
She waits in her cell.
The chains burn into her wrists.
Out, out is all she wants.
The fire cracks and hisses in her direction,
It doesn't register though.
She is gone.
Her eyes are black,
Holding no emotion.
With a small glisten you notice,
That nearly unnoticeable tear,
Slip out of the corner of her eye.
What have I done?
She smiles, knowing,
Her life is over.

Franceska Annemarie Kelley
*Spiro, OK*

## Me

Me, I am me, I think of myself as nothing more or nothing less
If I were to be someone different? I've never thought about it
I'd never want to change, even if I'm an idol for the rest
Would you want to be different, maybe totally opposite from you
Someone you manipulated anything you did, or even planned to do?
Or even someone you isn't like the other you
I wouldn't want to be anyone else even if I'm old and they're
  brand new!
I'll keep myself as I am, someone in this world loves you for you

Tori Renae Hooper
*Eldorado, OK*

*Poetry tells a story, from short to long. Every stanza is beautiful to me. I think poetry is a great way to pour your feelings out. I am sixteen years old. I've been in love with poetry ever since I can remember. I have a loving family that supports me in every situation, and for that I am blessed.*

# Can You Hear That Sound?

Can you hear that sound
The voices of the past
They scream and holler
From underneath the grass

Their corpses rot within the soil
Pulses halted, lives foiled
The tombstones tell their mortal stories
Born the eighteenth, died at forty

The cannon balls fire
Wounds covered in red
The smoke rises higher
As they are laid in their eternal bed

They fought for their loved ones
For the red, white, and blue
For freedom and honor
They died for it too

Their bodies now sleep
In rows of white marble
Though the willows do not weep
In fact, they are humble

Can you hear that sound
The voices of the past
They yell out in spirit
"Freedom at last"

Savannah Sue Craft
*Bradenton, FL*

*Now being an eighteen-year-old college freshman at my local community college, it is astounding to reminisce and see how well I was writing almost three years ago when I originally wrote this poem. I have always aspired to inspire others and I hope I can always do so.*

## Alas Another Season

Brisk air, gray sky
I sit with a tear, I am numb inside
I look upon an awesome sight
A city embellished in mortar rising out of the water
A city man has created
Deafening noise is the back, litter and garbage strewn around
I sit with a tear, I am numb inside
As I look and ponder
My life is crumbling too, dear Lord
Like some of the commandments you carved upon the stone
Moral decay, lying, drug euphoria, adultery, killing, and stealing
Man is tempting and daring you to send your Son Jesus Christ
If we spit upon and crucify Him again, slay us with total destruction
For we have destroyed ourselves within
I sit with a tear, I am numb inside
My life is in turmoil
I live with and love my husband more today than yesterday
He tells me he loves me more, yet, I doubt his word and action
I do not know why
Is it because of the world around me
Is it because of my self-doubt and self-worth
After a century I know not truth from lie
I sit with a tear, I am numb inside
Yes dear Lord, you are the creator of hope
Please send us an omen, an omen of hope
That my life and the life of the world
Will change and become the beautiful, beautiful
World you have created

Betty Shlepr
*Melbourne, FL*

## Beauty

I'm eager for the time we will have together
I wish I could make this last forever
You are so delicate, soft and young
I smile with joy now that our night has begun
I admire your skin all tender and silk
A natural beauty, as pale as milk
I play with your hair, so curly and blond
Immediately, your wonderful eyes respond
They sparkle with life and naïve emotion
As my hands caress your neck in one swift motion
I've never felt quite like this before
You play with my mind, and now I want more
You feel the same way, I notice you swoon
How weak I'm making you gets me over the moon
Such a strong feeling, I admit it's hard to cope
But I think I've found the solution, I hope
Before I can blink, your state has been shifted
Your eyes are now dull and your gaze has been lifted
But your face is still gorgeous, I can't help but check
As I release my firm grip on your fragile neck
I have to admit, I'm sad with the outcome
The task was too easy, you're quick to succumb
I lack satisfaction, I think with a sigh
But I stand by my beliefs, all beauty must die

Julia Marin
*Burlington, Ontario*

# Growing Up Today

In a room full of many things, I have many dreams
To grow up and be something, see many things

Growing up is not a joke though;
you have to do many things like talk correctly

Oh these things may be far from me;
growing up seems like an easy thing

You walk and you talk like a simple child would do,
but being grown up is a hard thing to do

When you're feeling sick you can't just lie down;
you must finish the things you are doing in town
But you can stay up late and eat what you want,
even though it's at your cost

Growing up is not what it seems;
you have to do many things
Pay bills, go to work, and even read

I want to grow up now and that's what I'll do;
I'll put on your fancy church shoes

No one said growing up was fun
In a room full of many things, you have many dreams
This too shall pass through your dreams;
sleep now you have many things to do
Because you have a lot of growing up to attend to!

Rachael C. Hollis
*Kellyville, OK*

## Untitled

A shadow
A ghost in my mind
Hidden among other shadows
This shadow, however, is different
Impossibly so
Hiding so purposefully
But, every so often
It will pass a mirror
It is then that I will see a glimpse
A color
Then one day
It does something different
It walks to a mirror, and stares
As if staring into its own soul
As if into mine

Hannah Simmons
*Hershey, PA*

# All Wrapped Up

The package does not always show the contents of
that which is within.
That pretty wrapping, and that pretty bow of the contents
it does not show.
We are the package the body is the shell.
Dressed, and painted with all that makeup.  For
the story you have to tell.
You live your life like an open book, for everyone
to see and read.
The rules of life you rejected, and God's word you
paid no heed.
When your life expires, and the book of life is opened
to your page, will you be satisfied with how you
lived in your shell, or will you gnash your
teeth in rage.
Oh the choices we are faced with.  If only we could
see ourselves as others do.  To change the bad behaviors
while there's still time before our final days are through.
To live as God intended—to worship him, and our
neighbors as well.
Maybe the world would be a better place before
the shell is empty, and you're bound for hell.

Brion L. Morse
*Silver Springs, NV*

*Although I enjoy reading poetry, writing was never an interest until my youngest
daughter was incarcerated for drug related issues. At that time, a poem was
included with a letter. Her cell mates loved my poems and dubbed me the Red Neck
Poet. An equipment operator and truck driver for most of my adult life never left
a lot of time for writing, but it did allow plenty of time to think. So although
dangerous, many poems were written behind the wheel while driving. Thanks for
the interest. Keep reading. Words have power.*

## Loneliness

Hearing all the conversations in the room, but no one hears you
Someone asking, "How have you been?" when you don't even
   have a clue

Being at the top only to fall once more
Looking to the sky asking, "What's this life for?"

Desperately seeking a bond between you and your very own child
Remembering days past when life was going with a smile

Giving to those who take kindness for weakness
Hearing a hollowed voice solemnly say, "We can beat this"

Always feeling defeated and being kicked while you're down
But keeping the faith until the answers are found

Closing your eyes and gasping for air
That's when you know that loneliness is there

Laurie Beth Carson
*Jackson, GA*

*This poem is dedicated to the loving memory of my mother, Christine O. Carson, my caring aunt, Connie Colwell, and my most precious and beautiful daughter, Hailey Christine Carson. My heart overflows with the love and gratitude I have for these three amazing ladies.*

# Came Upon a Dream Today

So... I came upon a dream today and a
poet was my muse. He told me tales of ships with
sails, and the oceans and all their blues. I came
upon a dream today and a poet became my friend
He told me rhymes and of histories times and
fretted for the end. I came upon a dream today
and a poet was my guide He said these simple
instructions before he'd let me ride. I came upon
a dream today and a poet was my teacher. He asked
of loved ones close to me and said I'd never
reach her. I came upon a dream today and a
poet was my foe. He spoke some lines, I redefined,
sent him packing lines in tow. I came upon a dream
today a poet was my reflection. I saw the mirror
and had to ask, why with the deception? I
came upon a dream today and the poet he is me.
And in my dream I seek the means to set my
own self free.

John Alton Warren
*Dearborn Heights, MI*

### Evergreen

At what age did I find myself?
Where? When?
Was I evergreen
between
the ears?
Was it then? Or in
later years—
when slick as a river rock,
fast as
seconds slipping
past on
a clock.
Was it then? I can't recall.
I only know it was yesterday if
at all...

Gary Warner Kent
*Austin, TX*

# Living with My Son As a Gang Member

My son was born
He was that perfect child
He was a joy
He was my son
When he turned thirteen
Everything about him changed
He killed anyone
He killed everyone
There was no mercy
He just killed
He bought guns
He sold guns
He bought drugs
He sold drugs
Every day was a nightmare
Every day was a killing
I had a nervous breakdown
Because every day was
The same

Jacqueline Ann Hayes
*Stockton, CA*

## Life's Storms

Each day the storm is becoming stronger and stronger, the waves are roaring with anger.
My ship can barely stand afloat.
The sails are torn to shreds for there are many worries and dreads.
The anchor only seems to take hold for short periods of time and just before I take my next breath I've been uprooted once again.
Each time is faster and faster it seems like such a crime.
The wind is blowing harder and harder, my ship is longing for a peaceful chime. Wandering, wandering how long will we have to keep scraping for a dime.
The structure has many holes but I keep pushing through and patching them along the way.
For I have belief that tomorrow shall bring a better, brighter, much calmer day.

Chanda Smith
*Cleveland, GA*

# A Poem for My Grand-Daddy

You were a strong man; never seen you shed a tear,
Through your sickness and struggles, you showed no fear.
I watched you everyday, you never ceased to amaze,
You knew a little about a lot of things in your days.
No matter what we needed, you were always right there.
Always offering to help, so we knew that you cared.
Between your words of encouragement and advice,
Paying you a visit was always nice.
You sung a lot of songs, and the jokes you would tell,
Those songs weren't real, though you sung them so well.
You were a man of your word, well known and loved.
I know you're watching us from up above.
You were a hardworking man, a great father and friend,
Who knew that all would come to an end.
You will be missed, will always be on our mind,
The best grandfather I could ever ask for,
You were definitely one of a kind.

Jalen Matthews
*Warren, MI*

## Terza Rima in Iambic Pentameter

Release your voice and speak to me in truth
Permit me not to suffer in this night
To give false hope would truly be uncouth

Once kind, my vision has become a blight
Please pluck my eyes from me and make me blind
No longer can I bear this curse of sight

Who knew that you so lovely, so kind
Could cause my heart unbearable torment
And shatter every fragment of my mind

One soul has never known such discontent
Nauseating pain no man should abide
And now I fear I must begin descent

Into madness without you by my side

Zachary C. Smith
*Baltimore, MD*

# Life Is Short

My life is like a volcano
It might erupt any second
I wake up every morning
Everything planned out to the minute:
Get up at five a.m.
Out of the house by seven
Get there at eight
Be home by nine p.m.
I go to bed every night wondering
If this is all there's left to life?
I wake up every morning and go straight to the schedule
To repeat everything over and over!
I go to bed every night wondering
If I'll wake the next morning
I'm a ticking bomb
With only a matter of seconds
Even with that, I still wake up every morning
Only to follow an absurd schedule
I go to bed every night regretting it
Hoping to get one more chance to make things right
I woke up this morning and skipped the schedule
Tonight I lay in a hospital bed knowing
I won't wake up tomorrow morning
But it'll be alright for I at least made things right
Life is short!
Don't wait as long as I did!

Christine Asatryan
*Tehachapi, CA*

## Lifetime Friends

A powerful first impression, that was genuine without any aggression.
A special presence with a colorful essence.
A strong bond from the start, just like a valuable piece of art.
Always knowing what's expected, both of us, mutually respected,
as we both were pre-selected.
Our personalities prominent, as we are both confident.
We both pay for our own ways, which guarantees all of our stays.
Eyes are hypnotizing,
Surreal and enticing.
All our actions, have never brought any bad reactions.
We had to part our separate ways, to met again in a few days.
At a new address, with more stories to confess.
A big embrace, would put a smile on our face.
A deeper level, our relationship went, all day and all night, well spent.
Long walks on beautiful redwood trails,
Our talks are honest, never tall tales.
What is said and what we do,
Our loyalties are always true.
Hearts are open and aware,
A trust that is beyond compare.
Again! We both had to leave, but would always believe.
We would definitely meet again,
Because, we will always be lifetime friends

Kerri Coplin
*Crescent City, CA*

*My name is Kerri Coplin. I am disabled and have been for twenty years. I have two grown children and two grandchildren. I have been married two times and am engaged at the present time to a wonderful man who saved my life. I grew up rough, was on my own at twelve years old, and lead an alcoholic and abusive life. I have overcome some severe obstacles and poetry has always been there for me. It's a chance to express myself in a way that someone might understand and helps me at the time I am writing the poem. "Lifetime Friends" was inspired by a male friend of mine that has shown me through the years that we are always going to be close, and that is unspoken, I just know. I have never had that especially with a male and it really means a lot to me. Heart just has heart, so does my poems. I hope and am grateful that you took the time to sit down with me and listen to what I have to say. Heart you have heart.*

# Colors of Change

Amber and azure hues infuse and diffuse
Over the jaundice chicken-like skin
From the morning daylight that is peeking through
The minimal thread count of the inexpensive sheets
Covering the window
The light weathered and stretched along my bruised limbs
From the wounds never quite healed
After this month's continuous battle
Tracks stretched and connected to the body
As if holding a purpose
To welcome these injections of dirt
Time cripples the senses with years
Of nonexistence, for the first time in a long time
I'm noticing a change all around me
A transcendence of seasons
A surpassing of space
An eclipse of an era in my life
And in the bodies that surround me
The redolence of the nectarous summer

Timothy James Kargo
*Portage, PA*

## In the Hours

In the hours
before the world awakens,
and I lose you

to the monotony
of need-tos,
haven't-yets
and must-dos

I lie awake,
listening to you breathe
in the darkened stillness.

Blanketed in safety
by your presence,
knowing you will return
only to me, I realize:

you are entirely mine
and I am yours, forever.

JC Chute
*Derwood, MD*

# Wind and Air

She drove the sea,
And he the sky.
He questioned her,
And she asked why.

He made the winds,
And she the waves.
He splintered woods,
And she made caves.

Unlikely friends,
They made a pair.
Wind and water,
Liquid and air.

Nicole Duchaine
*Richmond Hill, GA*

*My name is Nicole Duchaine and I am twelve years old. I have a very large family and I have three sisters and one brother. What inspired my poem was knowing how many things my grandmother does and there being no words great enough to say thank you.*

## A Letter-Perfect Birthday

C—hears the carols that add merriment to the happy scene;
H—sees the holly that decks the halls in shades of green.
R—is for Rudolph and the other reindeer that safely guide the sleigh;
I—welcomes the infant Jesus born to us today!
S—belongs to Santa and childhood memories;
T—stands for tinsel, trimmings and trees.
M—feels the warm, festive mood that can't be beat!
A—offers an Advent with preparation now complete.
S—pictures the stable where with loving arms unfurled...
    The Son came to be able to redeem a weary, waiting world!

Carolyn M. Lewis
*Little Falls, NJ*


*Carolyn remembers writing poetry for an eighth-grade assignment in the autumn of 1964. Her creativity was heartily acknowledged and thus flourished in a stable, loving home. The next fifty years found her increasingly aware of—and ever grateful to the Lord for—His tremendous blessing. She's honored that her prayerful poems still serve as the grace before special occasion family dinners. Always a lover of pomp and circumstance, Carolyn has "unwrapped" her "gift without a bow" countless times to warmly mark "smilestones" in her own and others' lives. May these lyrics be her legacy!*

# The Sea

Oh how is it now
The world sees me
As far from beneath the sea?
Oh simple wonder as I smile
To come up and smell the breeze

How can it be
That I must part
As once again I must dive
So far from all
And go beyond the touch
As I go beneath the sea

Someone hear me
And save me
From this dark and gloomy place
As I return, down, down
So far beneath the sea
Away from it all, as it takes me
Into the darkness where I cannot see

Down down where there is no path
A place I must find
A safe place for me to bind

Cleo R. Davis Frietze
*Mesilla, NM*

---

*This poem came to me one Sunday morning while I was waiting for coffee to brew. I was waiting for a cup of coffee before getting ready for church. So many times poems come into my mind and I don't take the time to write them down. I'm too busy with other things I enjoy. But on this Sunday morning, I could not ignore what was going on, so I found paper and I wrote it down. I have many other poems that come to me which I did write down, but somehow "The Sea" stayed with me.*

## Lost without God

Without God we will be lost, it will be
like riding on the wind going some place
but don't know where you are going or
which way to go, or on a ship that's
bound for nowhere, because if you go
west you don't know what's out there.
You will be lost if you go south, you will
be lost.  If you go east you will be lost.  If
you go north you will be lost.  You will be
just going in a circle.  Going somewhere
but don't know where you are going, but
with God you will always know where
you are going.  If you trust in the Lord
Jesus Christ, and keep God's word in your
heart always, the spirit of God will
speaketh into your heart — Matthew 10:20.

Always take the word of God with you
wherever you go.  Bind them continually
upon thine heart and tie them around
your neck.  When you go to sleep God will
keep you if you let the spirit of God lead
you, you will come to full knowledge of
which way to go.  With God you will never
go wrong.

Johnnie M. Turner
*Barstow, CA*

# Crescent Fall by the Weight of 5<sup>th</sup> Street

It's a jazz type feel pulsating through the floor
Enticing the soles of those who dance
In the midst of a Friday night frenzy where the couples are called
   to perform a trance
They swing and stomp
As the lady's heel adds to the rhythm of the saxophone
While many past at the bar guzzling whiskey for their lady left 'em
   all alone
As the jazzers swing in style, the blues crowd likes to drink
Notes from the stage are vibrating waves through the walls of
   where we cave
Under the roof of a gathering where Clementine brings us all to light
In the range of what his lyrics say
Driving a dagger to the essence of why we all round about here
Singin' hold your baby's hand tonight
For the rustle of her skirt may no longer be
When you propped up on a pedestal
Introverted just like me
Your whiskey tells a story
My trombone feels the sound
Of where your heart lay heavy
Bartender, order me another round
The tempo in his voice in unison with the weight on their minds
Abandonment felt through the strings that strum
Like a bucket of water sitting stagnant as a whole
Until poured down a stream of melodic flow
Escape from reality: life that you know
Stage crew lights the room
5<sup>th</sup> Street here we go

Sabrina Sacker
*Mustang, OK*

*I reside in Oklahoma City with a vision to inspire others through writing. Poetry for me is music livened by the tone of how the reader interprets it. My inspiration for creating this poem is to activate an element that makes a person feel happy through simplicity—all in the name of art. A connection far greater than what we would've ever dreamed can be attained by the communal sense of love just one piece of writing can create for many. Life lived through thought is the practice that makes those who internally feel like just a pebble, echo creatively to the whole bag of rocks. I hope you the reader enjoy this poetic verse to the extent that my intentions wished.*

## Wonderful "I" Words

With inspiration one's imagination rises
As if on the weathered wings of well-plumed ibises.
While lively words like icicles, irises and hives,
Inspire ingenious ideas of isotopes and ions.
Many important words find their exact opposites
By il, im, in and ir prefixes.
Ideas and imaginings once thought impossible,
With inclination and science are quite possible!
One need never be idle, there is so much to learn,
The more one knows, the more income one will likely earn.
"Infant" invokes images of idyllic delight,
While "infantry" instills thoughts of foot soldiers in flight.
An inquisitive child with intuitive mind
Might find his less curious forthright friends far behind.
Information gathering is a lifelong duty;
Find a lifetime of joy—aye, thrill in discovery!
Ideally chosen ideas illuminate the soul
One's path so directed will surely achieve life's goal.
"Integrity without knowledge is weak and useless,"
Vice versa, "is dangerous and dreadful," said Rasselas.
The prize of all prizes to win is intelligence—
God's infinite wisdom highly prized above all else.
It's important to guard against impulsivity,
While Immanuel guards the gates to immortality.
Please invite and incline towards kindly instruction,
One's mind and intellect might improve a micro fraction!

Alison M. Larsen
*Salt Lake City, UT*

*While studying children's literature at BYU and teaching for several years in the elementary grades, I learned to enjoy poetry, especially poetry written with children in mind, and to appreciate the talents of many remarkable poets.*

# Helping Hands

The farmer's hands are caked with soil
A mechanic's hand are slick with oil
They each know different kinds of toil
These are God's "helping hands."

The gentle touch of a mother's hand
The general's hand raised in command
A musician's hand that leads the band
These are God's "helping hands."

There are those hands that cause much grief
And others, of the common thief
Some make the joys of others brief
They should be "helping hands."

Lord, may my hands write happy songs
And strive, each day, to right a wrong
To spread some joy and love along
Please give me "helping hands."

Donna Marlene Pace
*Mannford, OK*

## Sage Advice to a Woman's Magazine Reader

Try meditating daily: take a garlic clove or two
Herbal teas, carrots and coconut milk are especially good for you
Take ginger in the morning, flaxseed oil at noon
Breathe deeply every chance you get: it will keep you quite in tune
Don't forget to think good thoughts:  to smile instead of frown
To floss, to flex, to strengthen abs, to wash up instead of down
Remember to visualize wellness, and to do it while drinking green tea
Remember to eat those soy products, and get plenty of vitamin C
After you have had all of your water—eight glasses, maybe nine
After you've done your deep-knee bends, you should be feeling fine
De-stress, de-tox, de-sensitize:  to your own self be true
Listen to soothing music or books on tape as you walk a mile or two
If you do all of these things daily, and a few more here and there
You'll extend your life by several years, but you'll be too tired to care!

Janet Dye
*Cable, OH*

# Soldiers

They died in the fields so far away
Not harvesting grain or making hay
Love, respect and honor for the USA
The dedication of life we can never repay
We can never pay that debt
It's one we ought not ever forget
We ought to remember those men and women
Everyday bow our heads in a loving way
Take some time to meditate and pray
There are also survivors with wounds to heal
They need our love and a better deal
The blood, the guts they have seen it all
Pinned down in a bunker wounded
And watching their comrades fall
We taught them to be killing machines
It's disgraceful to not supply their means
Those people ought not have to wait
For medical attention that comes too late
There is so much more to fighting a war
Than the gossip you hear in the grocery store
They faced the dangers
They should not be treated like strangers
They were the ones that made the sacrifice
You politicians worry about money
And you should not think twice
Shame on the ones responsible
They need to pay for being corruptible
Open the gates it may be a flood
They are the ones that sacrificed
And gave the blood

Don Rojem
*Moulton, AL*

## Life So Precious

A light blanket of snow covers the ground.  It covers the broken
earth that lays like the broken dreams and shattered hearts that
have been left behind.  The flowers we left will slowly fade and
themselves die.
As our pain and longing for you will slowly heal, but even as it
heals there will always be a piece of my heart that is missing
a piece that will always belong to you.
The world refuses to slow down, mocking the grief and pain that I
feel.  I just want the world to pause and acknowledge the work
That you'd done, the life you lived, the people you touched.
Pictures and memories more precious than the crown jewels give
testament to you and your accomplishments.
Visiting your graves and seeing your pictures on the stone give me
some comfort.  A place here on earth.  But I know you are no
longer here.  Heaven called you and you answered becoming angels
that still watch over and guide me from above.

Julie A. Salsido
*Imlay City, MI*

# I Am Proud to Be an American

From sea to shining sea
As Americans we are free
And I am proud to be an American

From the mountains to the hilltops,
Through the skyscrapers,
Over the rooftops
I am proud to be an American

From California to New York
Every casino, every resort
I am proud to be an American

From cities to the farmlands
From the CEOs to the farmhands
I am proud to be an American

Everywhere I go
Everything I see
I can truly say,
I am proud to be an American

Deborah Windwood
*Warren, OH*

*My name is Deborah Windwood. I have been writing poems most of my adult life. I am single and a born-again Christian. I am very, very patriotic. I love my country and my God. Everything in my apartment is decorated in Americana. I firmly believe in supporting my country, America, and my God, in whom I fully trust. I don't have a computer so I print everything—this is one thing I wish to purchase: a laptop and printer. This way I can go online with all my fellow poets. I wish everyone the best and encourage others to write poetry as well. I thank everyone and I do hope I have a chance to use my God-given talent.*

## Broken

Broken ship out at sea
Broken heart waits for thee
Broken shells upon the shore
Broken dreams for me no more

Broken home and broken wishes
Broken me with cups and dishes
Broken windows and broken lights
While water drips from broken pipes

Shall you return from the sea
To fix the broken barn and fence for me?
Restring the broken rod and reel
Take me fishing keep your deal?

The fridge is broken and the fryer
The washing machine and the dryer
The bikes, the tractor, and tools broken too
The mirror reflects I'm broken without you

The children wait with arrows and bows
A bandaged knee and runny nose
To play with toys and throw some balls
Push the swing and tea party with dolls

The roof is broken, moonlight shines through
Thoughts of promises and vows with you
As I cry, the seagulls sing this song to me
Of ocean waves on the sand, soon, returning thee

Diane Davis
*Orosi, CA*

# The Gift of Peace

Peace is slippery and elusive and very hard to find.
It dwells deep within your heart,
Hardly ever on your mind.
Peace is a very special gift that is given
To us from God above.
This great big package is wrapped with
Much care and given to us with love.
As eager, impatient children we open the gift and find:
Joy, long-suffering, gentleness, faith, love, temperance,
And a blessed peace of mind.
To accept this gift the sounds of the world,
Must all disappear,
So that the whispering of God, we can hear.
For peace is not found in conditions nor possessions that
The world wants to give
But is found in our daily walk with God
And how we choose to live.
Even though peace is elusive,
It can be found and truly attained;
If we will accept this great gift in our
Heavenly Father's name!

Betty Pickens Brown *Thaxton, MS*

## Margie

She's a daughter of the hills
Beautiful in every way
A little white hepatica haunting the glades
Shy as the deer-tongue lily in shady places

She is strong like the slender hickory
Faithful as the redbuds and dogwoods
That bloom in the spring
She is Margie

She's a spring of running water
At the bottom of the hill
Loving, nourishing those around her
Loved by those who know her

She is sometimes illogical
She loves me and she loves the snow
She blesses me always
Just because she is uniquely Margie

And she is mine

Robert Deatherage
*Yakima, WA*

## Notta

Notta is nothing,
If you trip over notta,
You'll never fall.

Ryan M. Sanders
*Houston, MS*

## Harmer's Choco Pie

When I eat a piece of Harmer's
Chocolate pie
I'll tell you the truth — I would not lie
The angels in heaven are singing
I hear bells — ringing
Lovely maidens are dancing
Lil elves are prancing
All's right with the universe
When they take me away in a hearse
I'd appreciate it, when I die,
If you'd slip me a piece of
Harmer's choco pie

Maxine Wilkerson
*The Villages, FL*

# A Talk with God

While sitting at my desk one lonely day
I asked the Lord if He was the only way
For me to have love, joy and peace
And these are the words He said to me:
"You can have that and much, much more
Just let me through your heart's closed door
Not that door that's made of metal or wood
But the one in your heart which changes your mood
Not only will your love be everlasting and true
It will be shown in the works that you do
Not in the things you do to get a pat on your back
But those to help others with the things they lack
From helping the homeless put a roof on their head
Or lying a young baby on its very first bed
From feeding those with no money or food to eat
To smiling at strangers and the enemies on the street
Don't be ashamed to bend on one knee
For this is when you are  most closest to me
Doing these things as an unselfish task
Are the answers to the questions of which you have asked
So yes I am the way, the truth and the light
And by keeping my word, you are within my sight"

Emma L. Robinson-Kohlheim
*Atoka, TN*

*Emma is married with four children. She has been writing for sixteen years. She enjoys meeting people, singing in her church choir and reading in her spare time. Her writing is inspired by events in her life as well as church sermons, family and friends.*

# 9-11-01

Early that morning, without any warning,
Our nation was thrust into shock and mourning.

Terror came at us out of the sky.
Most had no chance to tell loved ones good-bye.
The devastation—a horrible sight,
Casting thousands into an endless night.

Many are missing, others no more,
Anger wants to even the score.
Faith and praying is uniting all who are waiting.

Clarice M. Todd
*Grand Terrace, CA*

## Paper Lantern

flame
in a box—
a licking star, curling
the edges
like a burnt rose...

Joh Cambilargiu
*Tooele, UT*

*In writing this piece, I went back to a place of incredible energy, bursting out, strips of color and light run through my mind like a ribbon... flashes of ineffable beauty, and peace.*

# The Words of Many

Sitting in silence
The world speaks of peace
I think of how it would be
If you were to speak

The words of many
Including I
All it is… is Hi

Typing to you in silence
I wonder why
The words I speak
Go unnoticed
As if the page is blank

When

The words of many
Including I
All it is… is Hi

Walking along
I pass you by
Seeing into each other's eyes
I give you my smile
With no exchange
While all I ever wanted

Were
The words of many
Including I
All it is… is Hi

Tonya M. Barton
*Flint, MI*

# A Love Still Standing

In the beginning we had passion and fire, smoke and steam,
A love so bright the flames could be seen.
I will always believe in the magic of love because I will always
believe in the magic of us.
Our flame may not be quite as bright but, the spark still burns
long, deep and is oh so right.
We've been together for the past five years; we've survived the ups
and downs,
Gone through the happiness and tears.
We've shared our lows and highs, even when we tried to keep
them inside.
It was hard for me at first to trust and let you in but, my heart
realized that you were my friend.
I was in love with you in 1973 and I know in my heart that God
meant you for me.
So many trips we have taken together but, our greatest journey
will be
Forever.
I've learned so much just being in your presence.
I feel your warmth, I see your heart for others, I know your sense
of calm,
even in the midst of a storm.
I trust your loyalty and I am amazed by the patience you display.
I give you my heart, I trust you with my love, I am loyal and
faithfully yours
Today, tomorrow and always.
A love like ours is rare and grand,
It's nice to know that it still stands.

Brenda Shropshire
*San Jose, CA*

# You Are That Love

Loving you, already
You are the love
That lives in my soul and heart
Warmness of the weather
Uniting us and uniting us
Without making notice of it
Endless love
You are that love

You are that love
Love does not have limits
No borders, no barriers
Passion, emotion, desire
This love in between us
Is pure and genuine
Inside that purity are you

You are that love
Sweet love, sweet love
Thinking on you 24/7
Thinking on you in the sunrise
Thinking on you in the sunset
With all my heart: thinking on you!

Lorena Llong
*Reynoldsburg, OH*

*I am Lorena Llong from Reynoldsburg, Ohio; I want to share with you the joy of my heart. Love touched my door and I feel alive, full of hope and happiness after years of sorrow and sadness. For the creation of this poem I was inspired by the love, affection and kindness received from tender and sweet love Mike Conrad. You appeared one day and since then in unparalleled ways you have made me feel more than wonderful, beloved, respected and full of happiness. You are my tender and sweet love. When we met, you told me you were different! Yes love, you are different, you are a poem of love. You are a unique man, full of details and tenderness. You are a man, those, who remain a few. You are that love, a thousand times sounded odd years expected. God bless you always, sweet Mike!*

# Just Ask Misses Hope!

You may wonder who I am as I travel from town to town.

Well I am Misses Hope and if you ever feel like throwing up your hands and saying I cannot cope, just ask Misses Hope.

Child let me tell you: I saw men and women with a rope around their neck dangling from tall old trees. Frightened furious as can be. I fell on my knees prayed to God please! Please! Help me.

I Misses Hope worked from sun up, to sun down scrubbing floors, cooking, mending, tending to other folks chaps, entertaining uppity folk, yes sir, yes madam without as much as a frown. But instead I just spend my day smiling, extending and lending a helping hand.

Yes I am Misses Hope! Been there, done that, beaten down, broke down, talked down. But thanks be to God, my will and determination! Misses Hope still stand.

So learn from me they can break my body but not my spirit, they may try to deter my dreams and aspiration, but they can't stop me from being free one day. My answer is no, no I must say I will be free some day.

Life is so much bigger than they, my eye is on my prize. I will keep reaching and climbing with each passing day. As I glance at my future and embrace it more and more each day.

Out of my weary past I still stand at last. Today I am still proud to say, yes, I am Misses Hope who's been there and done that.

Anne Bradley
*Oakland, CA*

# The Arrival of a Hero

Common man and mighty warrior all in one,
Like the soldiers of old he took up his weapons,
Ready to defend his native land from all who threaten
The King called his name the war is won.

The soldier looks and sees how few remain;
Every member is written on his heart;
He knows every man is in a better place from war's start
Valiant men came and fought, but none died in vain.

The brave man looked toward the distant shore.
Home is calling for its native son.
He lays down his sword and shield then ran toward the sun;
Land is near just a few miles more.

The mighty warrior steps down and feels alive;
Soon he is greeted with smiles and cheers;
His family cries joyous tears,
The crowd shouts and says, "Finally our hero has arrived."

Amy Proctor
*Beach Park, IL*

*I first started writing poetry in eighth grade for an English assignment. Our English teacher, Mrs. Warren, wanted us to write our own poetry notebook for the majority of the class, it was our first time writing poetry. Our teacher taught us several different poetic styles. I loved every minute of the assignment. I discovered I was actually pretty good at poetry and each poem was exciting. I continued to write poetry all through high school. I entered a poem every year for our fine arts competition. I am still writing poetry to this day and have only just begun!*

# The Way, the Truth, and the Light

I looked far and wide
And found nowhere to abide

Just when I thought life was at its worst
I found First Missionary Baptist Church

When I first came, it was for all the wrong reasons
God, changed everything, and made it my season

I met this man, who had a warm smile
He was laughing and talking all the while
With a warm welcome, it was Pastor James R. Dowell

He was like a breath of fresh air
It was like being at the state fair

He was like the light at the end of the tunnel
A man of God, in one joyous bundle

With a hands-on approach to the ministry
This man of God, has the right chemistry

He's concerned about all who come to worship
At First Missionary Baptist Church

If you have no place to belong,
Come to First Missionary Baptist Church,
And he'll make you feel right at home.

This is the place you want to be.
If you don't believe me, come and see.

Robert Matthews
*Cairo, IL*

## The Man That I Am

I am not a genius or doctor that's plain to see.
I'm just an old country boy from Tennessee.
I grew up on peas, potatoes, corn and corn bread.
Such things as T-bone steaks was above my head.

Over the years I have watched what people ate.
I have often said too much meat was a mistake.
If I had to choose between vegetables or meat
All the way to the garden would be my retreat.

It's which came first, the chicken or the egg
Why is cholesterol so high to the doctor, beg.
Some say I've got to have meat every meal
Got to have steak at least three a week their appeal.

George Eskew
*Huntingdon, TN*

# The Human Cloud

I am a human cloud
Can't scream but I'm so loud
Begging the real ones in the sky
Asking why's the valley so dry
Not feeding this thirsty crowd
My trees all look so lean
My yellow lawn's not green
All day I'm looking up
Holding my empty cup
Mother Nature is so mean
She knows that things won't grow
No tears that these clouds throw
With everything we need
For every crying seed
Hey where's my $H_2O$
Some things aren't in this town
That we would pass around
No swimming pool
Or hospital
Calexico's so down
So please try wet us all
And flower seeds that fall
They're all thirsty
Like you and me
And make my trees get tall
I am a human cloud

Juan R. Nogales
*Calexico, CA*

*Hi, my nickname is "Dog." In the past, I won a medal for the third fastest in a 100-meter breaststroke in California, and I played bass, wrote and sang in The Doomed. On December 15, 1994, my car was hit by another. My brain and skull were broken in half and I was in a coma. Doctors and schools brought me back to life. I wrote this poem to inform people of Calexico's problems. We need a pool to stay fit and a hospital to stay alive. Why can't people even be born in Calexico? I hope someday you'll hear the songs I wrote about the rest of my life.*

# Hope for the Heartbroken — Revelation

"Hello Jesus," as He took my hand in His.
"I'm so glad to see you. I didn't know if I'd make it.
I am such a sinner in thought, word, and deed
Every second, every minute, every hour, of every day.
I have tried though.
You told us to love our enemies, but I sure don't like them
And what they do! Also to bless them that curse you and
Do good to them that hate you and pray for them
Who spitefully use you and persecute you."
And Jesus replied, "Welcome home, my child.
Let me take you to my Father."
Looking around, it was very beautiful, perfect, and peaceful.
And there was God and Jesus said,
"Abba Father, this is one of your faithful children who has gone
Through many trials and tribulations."
And God said, "Glad to see you, my child.
They don't steal or trade up here.
Neither do they prowl around, covet, home invade.
They are not greedy, cruel, jealous or hateful.
There is only love. I am love."
Like John told us many times, "God is love."
Thank you God, Jesus, Holy Spirit for your
Love, grace, mercy, and justice.

Janeann B. Moody
*Wataga, IL*

## Love Got Me Here

Whenever life gets me down
I smile instead of frown,
because what my parents taught me.
Love from deep inside my soul,
I can release it and let it
bloom and grow, because love got
me here.
A happy place where I
can always come home to
I feel my heartbeat and
I know that I'm free.
Love got me here.
A place where I can always
be, by knowing God made my
parents and my parents (Gerald and
   Ruth Makovsky) made me.
Love got me here.

Susan Ruth McQuiston
*Everett, WA*

## Moving the Dunes

The wind has done its work
and polished
        the massive mounds
                into gently sloping dunes
yet
no danger of sunburn here.
The balmy double digits
do not overheat us in our task
for they begin with one.
A far cry from the temps of last evening
as particles
        stung our faces
           in the windy, moonless night.

The sun casts shadows
and we pause

to appreciate Mother Nature's sculptures
before we again
lean into our shovels

to move
        the white dunes
           of the snowdrifts.

Deborah Ward Hoglund
*Youngsville, NC*

# Quilt Butterfly

This little butterfly was once on a quilt getting very, very, worn.
It was about to be discarded for its edges were so ragged and torn.

But as I looked at all those butterflies and thought about their past,
I thought somehow I must save them. I'll recycle them so they'll last.

I thought of how much work it took to bring them into life:
The loving hands that cut and sewed them, no doubt a farmer's wife.

I can picture an old log cabin, her in a rocker beside the fire.
Making old feed sacks into a quilt by winter was surely her desire.

I can see her as she sorted those old sacks with such tender
  loving care.
Making sure she matched just the right colors to her quite a fanfare.

She spent many long days sewing all those butterflies into just the
  right place.
And when her quilt was all finished, I can see the pride that was
  upon her face.

Not only had she made a bedcover that would many years keep
  them warm,
She had created a butterfly garden, her bright spot in the old cabin
  there on the farm.

Now, from that old quilted garden where they had never been alone,
I've cut them free from each other to fly away on their own.

So create your own bright spot somewhere within your home.
By placing this little butterfly there, and no more shall it roam.

Sandra Krull
*Hermann, MO*

*My inspiration for writing "Quilt Butterfly" came from an old quilt that was
given to me. It was made with blocks of appliquéd butterflies. The blocks were
still in good shape but the material they were set together with was falling apart.
Considering the time and effort it took to create that old quilt, I felt the need to
salvage what I could to pass on to future generations. I cut the blocks. The poem
I wrote and gave them as gifts to family and friends.*

## Someone Whom I Knew

Someone whom I knew
Was as great as could be to me
Someone who has been true to me
From this point on forever I see
He will always be a great friend to me
Someone whom you can trust, doesn't stand a fuss
He knows what the deal is between me and him
Pleasant at all times and loves to tell me I'm fine
And kind and I blow his mind
Wants me always to be looking nice
He would like to see me get married
And he will provide the rice,
So sweet and creative
And has a wonderful sense of humor
Loving, caring and sharing —
A person who never spreads rumors
He is someone special to me and my life
And I could have been his wife;
But I chose not, he was just a great friend to me
As greatest as could be
Who could rock your world if you wanted to see
Who was he? Someone whom I knew

Stephanie Rena Luke
*Phenix City, AL*

# Between Heaven and Earth

I await to see the promised land
I wait for long hours of my day
I view my reflection in the mirror, to find the lines of
time creasing my brow
I glance above my head
I see the salt and pepper of time touching my hair
A tear develops in the corner of my eyes; the flood
erupts into my linear cheeks
My dream all suddenly disappears before the image
on the mirror
How can you stop the sands of time from its course?
How can you stop a being from existing, a mass
whose soul remains floating aimlessly in time forever
At last my dream has come
This life that I so jealously embrace is about to
embark on a journey to that promised land, oh the
whiteness of the clouds caressing my body,
magnitude of space, oh pearly gateway high above
the bliss, weightiness of space, caressing my
being so long life, I bid adieu

Nelva Concepcion
*Bronx, NY*

*I write because my love of writing comes from within. My mom passed on September eleventh, 2014. I dedicate my poem to my mom. Her name was Julia Garcia Ithier. May she rest in peace.*

## Blue

She wasn't much to look at, kind of rough and dingy too
Her coat was somewhat mottled, with eyes a startling blue
She looked at me and seemed to say, please mister give me a chance
I couldn't turn and walk away from that puppy's glance

I picked her up and there she was, just a rack of bones
I thought that I could sure do right to give this pup a home
I mounted up my tired horse and headed for the house
The puppy snuggled in my arms was quiet as a mouse

The days went by and turned to weeks and how that puppy grew
She got me laughing time and again, and I would call her Blue
I caught her one day while at play, the chickens in a bunch
And thought about her herding hens, and then I had a hunch

I took her with me to the herd, my daily chore to feed
And when I rode around the cows, Blue's eyes would shine with glee
Bit by bit we worked it out, and the chore became a game
I would work around the cows and she would do the same

A yip, a bark, and then a growl, she knew which way to go
Watching her work the cows that way was really quite a show
The years went by as they will for me and my dog Blue
Not only a great cattle dog, she's my best friend too

Tammy Yeakey
*Ellensburg, WA*

## Stand in Truth

What should one do when problems face us?
Should we go face to face to the problem—
By first putting on one's game face, face to face,
Or should we go faceless, whilst facing the music?
Let's face it whether one puts on a good face or
A bold face no amount of face cards can truly face the
Matter or face the facts when a problem faces us!

Best to face up to the face off
Even though it may mean a smack in the face
Which could lead to a face ache
(To soothe simply fill face cloth with ice)
To lose face to another person's face—
Does not equal face value
But encourages us to put a new face on
And not face anyone about—
But rather, look persons in the face of a problem
And sense a face lift—no matter what we are faced with
Or in the face of—don't set one's face against doing so
Since it's not like one would be removed from the face of the earth

Peta-Gaye Vernon
*La Jolla, CA*

*Peta-Gaye Vernon enjoys writing poetry and children's stories. This will be her first appearance as a published poet.*

## The Gift

How dare I choose to compete
with death and old age.

Maybe that's the best way
to enter this phase.

Perhaps lack of acknowledgement
chases them from the stage.

But reality kicks in, and all
end in an unforgiveable maze.

Some mortal so-called messengers
from Heaven,

Will guarantee a spot there for
a generous stipend.

But in the end, science, the
universe, and the beautiful earth,

Will reclaim the gift of life
after your years since birth.

Janice Pazienza
*Mount Pocono, PA*

*I have a daughter and son, Tracy and Bruce Van Brakle, two grandchildren, Kate and John Jackson, and my husband Martin Romanchick. I'm fortunate to have such a bright and loving family! As a small child, I developed great interest and inspiration in the natural treasures around me in the mountains of Pennsylvania. This has always stayed with me, and I shared it with the children in my classrooms and at the environmental center where I worked after retiring from teaching. Finally, I respect all religious beliefs which are not misrepresented by human interpretation. Spirituality also exists in nature.*

# Sailing the Sea of Life

Each must sail his ship along and brave the sea of life.
We each must roll with the angry waves of prejudice and strife.
I fashioned myself a liner — beautiful and brown,
'Twas a magnificent sight — I guarantee until it went aground!
Its hull was scarred, its banner torn, and I in my dismay
Gave it up for a schooner and a little extra pay.
The schooner I chose was a hardy ship; it gave me quite a thrill,
Until a fire broke out in the boiler and its value they said was nil.
I patched her up and painted her — she didn't look too bad —
But a hurricane the next day, took all I ever had!
I admit this with regret — I thought the sea was against me,
Couldn't sail it on a bet!
Thank God I found a fallen tree — and with rocks and sweat and fire,
I fashioned me a small canoe — and floated above the mire!
I haven't given up that "dream" I had — fact is, I'm still dreaming.
But I do it now a day at a time — without that powerful "scheming!"
I've learned to roll with the angry sea and live life at its best.
God will guide my wandering soul — I feel sorry for the rest.
They, in their infamous glory of "dog eat dog — and lust,"
Lack the tranquil beauty, of God, of family, and trust!
I'll make my way as best I can down the sea and toward the ocean.
My scars have healed, my course is set —
My cargo, "love and devotion."
The past is now behind me, and I've learned a little "trick."
Roll with the waves that would cut you down —
And help those you see, "sea sick."

David E. McDonald
*Panhandle, TX*

## Hopes

"Read me a story, Mommy," my little girl says each day
As she comes and leans against me, when tired of her play.

As we reach up and take from the shelf her treasured
Storybook friends,
I look at her eager face and hope that her love of
Books never ends.

For, I have heard said many times in my life —
'Tis a saying I fondly cherish.
You need never be bored if you learn how to read,
And, an active mind will not perish.

You can fill your thoughts with garbage,
Cram with useless information
Or set your goal from the start
To get a good education.

But, if you can read the printed word
And learn to sort the good out,
And put it all to its proper use —
You'll succeed in life without doubt.

Ellen R. Connie Frost
*Watertown, NY*

# The Day the Laughter Died (Good-Bye Robin)

Once there was a song about "the day the music died."
  Why is it the most gifted burn out so fast?
So many sad hearts and so many tears cried,
  At least with film the legend will last.

Depression and addiction can be so misunderstood.
  Those who have it feel ashamed and try to hide it
If we could bring it out of the shadows as we should
  Beware all those who judge, you could be the next hit.

We see veterans, jobless, homeless and confused
  Some also have mental problems
Some are afraid and end up abused
  And they feel that there's no one to help them.

We're so sorry you decided it was time to go
  Your smile healed so many hearts, but not your own.
We'd bring you back if wishing would make it so
  But wishes are for dreamers and you were alone.

Maybe you heard the voices inside your head
  Maybe the angels needed you to make them laugh.
Whatever it was, it took you away from us instead
  And nothing can change what has come to pass.

You left us with laughter and smiles
  And we'll say good-bye with our tears and prayers.
We know your friends walked that final mile
  So just glance back with a smile, climbing the stairs.

Juanita Uransky
*Norfolk, VA*

# Why Did Some Die

was it simply luck of the draw or something as complex
as collecting and paying dues why could some go home and forget
while others are still crying and I just went crazy for a year
or two or was it five why did some become junkies
some through a needle others up the nose
some smoking dope continuously others not at all
why did some stay drunk others drinking not a drop
some only in town
why were some in dangerous locations others in no danger
and I in between
why did some break down in the midst of it all
others showing no emotion while I laughed then
and cried later
and more than twenty years after why am I still asking
why did some die but not I

Dail Edward Chaffin
*Broaddus, TX*

*I started writing in 1967, but I only showed my work to my sister and any woman
I was dating. In 1988, a girl named Che'Brock gave me the title after three trips
to Vietnam. During the third trip, my captain noticed I was drinking a lot and
getting into fights. He offered me an honorable discharge for medical reasons.
After some years of fighting and drinking, I got help and went to college. Working
toward my first degree in human services, Che'Brock introduced me to small press
between 1988 and 1992. I had over one hundred pieces published. My second degree
is an AA in human services and my third degree is a BSW. Finally, by 1999, I got
my master of social work and I became a child abuse investigator. I retired and
now write and take care of my mother and brother.*

# As You Walk By

I brought you flowers, all pretty and bright
You love them so much and wanted them just right

In Heaven's garden, you'll be the one to groom
All those beautiful blossoms, that forever bloom

And when on my balcony I work and toil,
Planting flowers, working my soil

I'll shade my eyes and look to the sky
So give me a little wave as you walk by

For now I'll tend my garden and watch it grow
While up in Heaven you will surely know

That you're forever in my heart
These flowers will remind me that we're never far apart

When I am sad and miss you so much
I'll tend the flowers still warm from God's touch

So don't forget as I raise my watering can high
Look below as I look to the sky
So give me a little wave as you walk by

Martha Martin
*Sacramento, CA*

# Life Goes On

Halfway shattered
At the breaking point
In rags that are tattered
Sore at the joints

Tired and sad
Maybe angry or mad
But still alive
And ready to thrive

90 percent given up
10 percent determined
Some people see me and say, "What's up?"
And I don't say a word and

This is how I live
Even though some people would give
To be me
But right now I feel as small as a flea

Nobody cares
They just walk by
I feel like I'm caught in a snare
And nobody asks, "Why?"

But I'll still try
Try as I might
People will ask, "Why?"
Because my heart's taken flight

Jacquelyn R. Torres
*Stoughton, MA*

*My name is Jacquelyn R. Torres. I'm thirteen and live in Massachusetts. I wrote this poem in sixth grade when I was eleven in my S.T.E.M. engineering class (not one of my favorites); I got bored and started writing a poem. The poem is about finding yourself in a bad place and not knowing how you got there. It's about overcoming self-loathing and getting yourself back on track. When I wrote the poem, I wasn't happy and writing it made me feel better. As for inspiration, I didn't have any but my own thoughts and feelings.*

## It Was an Autumn Wind

It was an Autumn wind.
It was the way that the wind *was* —the way it *twisted* and *curled* and
  *wrapped* and *enveloped*.
Crisper than Summer but softer (lessfrighteninglesscruel) than
  Winter.
It was like a brief hand to the cheek sitting outside alone with a
  book bubbling excitementinthefaceofanewadventure*climbinga-
  mountainandgettingtothetop*.
It was a Fall wind.
Or, rather, what the Fall wind would be.
It was as if it was sitting right behind the Summer breeze, in the
  place where seasons went, waiting to come sweeping in.
If I could have just pulled —*notyankedorjerkedorwrenchedbutasoftslowtug* —
  at those orange and brown tendrils of moving airoxygencolorlife
  then fall would have pushed past summer and froze everything
  that summer grew and shifted *proudly* in place because of (*notin-
  spiteof*) coming early.
It was a fallAutumn wind.

Sarah McLellan
*Salisbury, MA*

## Power

This little thing called power
Can undoubtedly go a really long way.

Even today, if we're not careful we,
though intelligent, can land in the gravel.

History, in itself, speaks quite plainly
about our rise and fall to power,

Power's corruption of individual willpower
is all too evident.

Since time corruption the individuals
who fought endlessly for our freedoms, at
this very moment, have a block of cement,
Standing at their ovation of individual willpower
that even stands after death at this very hour.

Since, individual willpower was not lost
but gained clearly shows in the continuing power
of patriotism.

This is true power which
continues to grow endlessly, and will for
generations to come.

Virginia Cline
*Waverly, OH*

## Thirst

My mind is swollen as a mother in gestation.
I revel in secrets hidden in my past.
My conscience swells with values of right and wrong.
I feel lost.
Locked outside my person.
Looking in, but still not being able to see.
A million songs I have caged inside my head.
I lay my body down for much needed rest.
Spirits of persecution haunt me even as I sleep.
They take away my only sweet comfort given in a dream.
The thirst of love is real.
It can never be quenched by just one.
My soul is an oasis from which all men drink.
Let my reservoir flow.

Vickie Walton
*Reynoldsburg, OH*

## Kitty on the Prowl

She prowls her jungle on small quiet feet,
through still gray mist with her body crouched low,
like a deadly panther from Mozambique,
her eyes alight with the moon's pale glow.
The night is full for a creature of prey,
with danger to face and shadows to explore,
she leaps at something in the grass where it lay
and startles it with her jungle-cat roar.
She listens to the night and sniffs at the breeze,
swaying to the beat of the night's strange tune,
climbing to the top of gnarled old trees
to talk with the wind and stare at the moon.
She searches the dark with soft yellow eye,
trembling at the sound of night things' cry.

Dennis J. Campbell
*Farmington, NM*

# One Lone Leaf

One lone leaf clinging to a branch,
Quivering in the breeze.
How strong must the wind be
To bring you to the ground,
To join the countless other leaves,
That failed to hang on?

Mary Jane Petersen
*Denison, IA*

# My Daddy's a Cowboy

My daddy's a cowboy, and I know that is true, because every day
he eats all his stew.

He rides all around on his beautiful horse and acts like he's in an
obstacle course.

He builds fences and likes to play ball, and I know that he knows
it all,
and sometimes he lets me bat or put on his dusty old cowboy hat.

I know that he loves me, I know that is true because every night he
says, "I love you."

Emily Laub
*Humansville, MO*

## Ode to the Crock-Pot

It's not the shape of your pot that begs,
Nor the length of your hollowed stubby legs.
Can it possibly be your lengthy cord tail?
I know! It must be your slow methods that prevail!
I do appreciate your helping hand
I can leave you for hours and return to a meal so grand!
You can turn tougher meat... chuck roast... stew meat... into
something so tender
Anything that the fridge or freezer should render!
At first we pray and give thanks to Him,
As the Crock-Pot awaits just filled to the rim!
We talk about our day and all that we've learned,
For we are always so thankful another meal is earned.
We discuss at our meals our possible new endeavors
Along with our life's most simple pleasures!
We love to have guests at our dinner table...
Would have it every night if someone were able.
The laughs and smiles during meals are the best
At times, certainly puts our manners to the test!
Oh, how we enjoy our meals together...
Try to eat slowly knowing the pot won't last forever.
We thank you for all the years of pleasantry
Sure helps me avoid kitchen dilemma insanity!
Oh Crock-Pot... how you make cooking at ease.
Lots of ingredients and sure to make the family say, "More please!"
However I fill you, with whomever I share,
You betcha you'll be present in my next cooking affair!

Katherine J. Prest
*Waukesha, WI*

*My poem describes my family's lesson of unity—not only for the love that surrounds cooking, yet to include the joy and importance of foundation within a family. "Family dinner" was a tradition we shared with a crew of six children which continues today with our individual families. We too are thankful for Him and will always cherish our mother's love in the kitchen! My next endeavor is to publish her cookbook that all six of us own, titled,* Mom, How Do Ya? *Always in memory, I hold it up to the heavens and give thanks each time.*

## Flickering Lights

Pumpkins aglow
Their flickering lights
Scary faces
Shining through the darkness
On this Halloween night

Casting shadows on the moon
Oh no! Are we all doomed

With witches and warlocks
And creepy ghouls
Kittens, dragons, butterflies too!

Feeling the magic in the air
Floating without a care
And black cats on the prowl
In downtown sleepy Howell

The headless horseman
Takes a bow
Sending shivers
Down to the bone
Out in the darkness
You're not alone

With pumpkins aglow
Their flickering lights
Shining through the darkness
On this Halloween night

Cheri Torbico
*Howell, MI*

# I See Beautiful

She stands in a trance of inspiring awe, hypnotized by the
sound of continual waves breaking along a tranquil shoreline…
each wave unique as it pulsates to its inevitable end.
Fine lines appears as whispers on a childlike face as she smiles
in appreciation of each wave come and gone. Chin up like a
flower reaching for the sun… kissed cheeks show the love of
ocean breeze and salt air. I see beautiful from sunrise to sunset…
hair tossed over bare shoulders, wide eyes playing with the
  shimmer of
the brightness of the day. Toes tickle white sand as she plays a silly
game in the warm surf. She kneels toward her reflection in a tide pool
and kisses the woman staring back at her. She laughs easily and it
says less of age and more of the beautiful soul of a woman.
She is art in motion, perched atop a ocean sprayed cluster of
worn stones… she's amazingly sensual, drenched skin in sweet oil
and the glow of her honeyed tan. Held close to me I see beautiful…
When apart I remember her on that day and I see beautiful…
Every wanted kiss returned to me, as she looks into my own eyes.
I see beautiful.

Eric Fuller
*Belle Vernon, PA*

# Expectation

What is it I want from you?
I don't know.
Maybe it's understanding.
Maybe not…
Perhaps it's just wanting you to acknowledge,
That I exist.
As me.

Catherine L. Crandall
*Medford, OR*

# Small Ponderings

I'm alone but don't feel lonely
It is dark but I'm not afraid
I'm not brave but I feel confident
For I'm in my final stage
I'm submerged but I'm not drowning
I'm compressed but don't feel squeezed
And I'm functioning quite perfectly
Even though I've yet to breathe
I am fed though my mouth's not open
I'm all warm like a hand in a glove
I'm a baby inside a womb growing
And I was conceived out of love

Lynn Kearns
*Monmouth Junction, NJ*

## Creation Elation

Do not shallow elation
Do not challenge creation
Do not rip the seams sewn us asunder
Deny truths and mute the thunder
Paralyze your pair of eyes
Or scream and curse His name

Don't ground the wheel till time stands still
Or pray a prayer with wicked will

Do not chain the sacred sayings
Do not halt the speech delaying
Responsive words, should not be heard
Don't grate the name degrading

Do not skin the naked men then bury them in foreign lands
Grains of sand, in different hands,
Would be much faster, in the end

The silver lining, blinding, shining
What lies behind is mystifying

Do not break, nor bend, nor bust
Do not lie, collecting rust
Do not fight, but when you must,
Fight for God, in Him we trust!

Jeremy Slone
*Warsaw, IN*

# We Don't Live in a Barbie World

We live in a world where society will find something
Wrong in everyone's appearance and doesn't care
About a person's worth
They tell you to be yourself
And that you're perfect the way you are,
But they also tell you that you're not good enough
Society has standards
Once you meet those standards, they come up with more
If you are not a toothpick then you are fat
If you are a toothpick then you have an eating disorder
There is just no winning their sick game
Last time I checked people don't come from Barbie boxes
We don't live in a Barbie world and it is *not* fantastic
We are flesh and blood not pieces of plastic
Society can't keep morphing their definition of perfect
These unrealistic standards can end people's lives
Society feeds on our insecurities
I was not born to constantly be told
That I'm not good enough
I was not born to please people or to look pretty
I was born to be happy

Megan Elizabeth Allen
*Miami, FL*

## End Times

These are the end of times,
my friend.
With each new day,
that's hastened in.
That day is close,
even at the door.
This world will soon,
be here no more.
And though that day,
is drawing near,
I look ahead,
and without fear.
For when that final,
day is come,
we'll see the coming,
of God's Son.

Tommy Randall Wigington
*Simla, CO*

## Women

captured by beauty
limited by design
seeing the skin
and nothing behind
eternally objectified
an agenda at best
a to-do list unfinished
an insurmountable quest

Kaitlin Horch
*Tampa, FL*

## The Floor

Perhaps
  it is the rolling
  or the pressing
  or the open space filled with possibility,
  or the contrast of soft on hard,
  or the feeling of being low to the ground,
  creature-like and primal.
Or perhaps
  it's just *us* —
  *any*time,
  *any*where…

Bernadette
*Bergenfield, NJ*

# When There Is Love

When there is love,
One has the world by the tail,
One can move mountains single-handed,
One's own heart will sail.

When one has love,
One can do most anything,
One can smile endlessly
One's happiness, they'll sing.

When your love touched me,
It made my heart feel ever new,
I now have the love from within,
I wish to always share it with you.

When one has love,
Like you've given unto me,
Their lives change so wonderfully,
Your love has set my soul free.

When there is love,
One can do most anything,
Let me give to you always,
My heart, my soul, my everything.

Teresa C. Whitney
*Mooresville, NC*

## Shopping Time

Ruby pumps shining there
Customers watching everywhere
Can't wait! It's shopping time
I've been saving every dime
Sale, sale, sale! Time to shop
Let me get my shopping cart
Prada candy perfume smelling good
Just like I imagined it would
OMG! I have eight bags!
I'm just steady ripping off price tags
Sale, sale, sale! Time to shop
Let me get another shopping cart
Walked into the beauty shop
Walked out looking as bad as a cop
Now I'm done, shopping time over
See the mall in the rearview mirror over my shoulder
Sale, sale, sale is over
Feeling luckier than a four-leaf clover!

Timia Shaffer
*Washington, DC*

*My name is Timia Shaffer. I am eleven years old. I have a big family and most of the time to visit them I have to fly on a plane. I live in Washington, DC, with my mom, sister, and my cousin. I'm the youngest but I don't mind. My aunt loves to take my cousin and I shopping. My sister and I always watch movies that have lots of old vintage designs in it. I was inspired. I wanted to make a poem and actually one day buy it. I wrote a poem about shopping.*

# Puppy Love

There is always room for "puppy love."
If you are big or small or even very tall —
There is always room for puppy love.
If all the loves we ever knew
Were as true as puppy love
We'd be in a happy place with puppy love.

Even beyond this puppy stage
Puppy love is all the rage.
They just go on loving you
With their beautiful, innocent
Puppy love.

So to someone I may just adore,
You're welcome to a great big bit of —
Puppy love.

For any time —
The sweetest gift
May simply be —
Puppy love.

Thelma Lash Payne
*Indianapolis, IN*

# My Mirrored Image

My life doesn't mean anything
Nobody will say
I wasn't a failure
People will tell me
That I wasn't worth their time
No one will say
I deserve to live
Those who love me will tell me
My words have no meaning
All who meet me will never say
That I am strong
I tell myself
I am not a burden
It is not true
I realize
All that they tell me
I choose to focus on
Why do I do that?
*(Now read from the bottom to the top)*

Holly May Baker
*Cincinnati, OH*

## Priceless

A sweet song,
A living spark.
Those are two,
But one at heart.
The sweetest song
As e'er was heard:
Hear it echo
Through the world.
Some call it hope's longing cry,
But I will name it Love:
A mother's heart, with gentle eyes,
E'en if her hands be rough.
This love rings in the city,
And echoes through all the land:
A love so great, it even lives
Inside a reprimand.
A mother's love is priceless,
In the city or the land:
No matter age or distance,
She's there to hold your hand.

J. B. Edwards
*Hudson, FL*

## Toyland

I'd like to return to Toyland
Where wishes all come true,
Where lullabies can heal the pain
And turn one's skies to blue;
Where lollipops and candy canes
Are on the bill of fare,
And Santa Claus makes his visit
When one is least aware;
When baby dolls and choo-choo trains
Are always in his pack,
And there's nothing but contentment
And childhood bliss to track;
Where every day's a holiday
And there is so much cheer
That your cup would runneth over
And last throughout the year.
If I could return to Toyland
Where childhood dreams come true,
I'd prefer to spend that childhood
With no one else but you.

Rosalie Smith
*Palmyra, MO*

*My favorite subject in school was always English, which included composition. I was chosen for the lead in the senior class play as well as a member of the committee to write the class history and to read that history at our graduation exercises. In my poem I dedicate that poem to a class member who has a doctorate in chemistry. I have not seen him since the night of graduation but he plans to come to see me next month. Thank you for choosing my poem for your anthology.*

# I'm a Millionaire

I believe in prayer, millions do
I'm a millionaire
My children said, we love you to a
Zillion times a million
I'm a millionaire
I have a job to meet my needs
I have friends who make me laugh with
Silly deeds, I'm a millionaire
The grass is mine and flowers too
The sky is mine with evening stars
My thoughts, my hopes, my dreams can soar
I'm a millionaire
My little dog has loved me with absolute trust
I'm a millionaire
Dance and music belong to me
My feet don't care if it's a samba or the rumba
I'm a millionaire
Be my friend and you will see just how
Rich our lives can be
We'll be millionaires, you and me

Peggy Travaille
*Aurora, MO*

# Index of Poets